The Journey of
DESIRE

Journal & Guidebook

An Expedition to Discover the Deepest Longings of Your Heart

JOHN ELDREDGE
With Craig McConnell

THOMAS NELSON PUBLISHERS®
Nashville

A Division of Thomas Nelson, Inc.
www.ThomasNelson.com

Published in Nashville, Tennessee, by Thomas Nelson, Inc.

Published in association with Yates & Yates, LLP, Literary Agents, Orange, California.

ISBN 0-7852-6640-2

Printed in the United States of America
02 03 04 05 06 PHX 5 4 3 2 1

To my father—"I've found our sword." It's bigger than I imagined.
To my wife, Lori—you are simply beautiful.
And to our daughters, Lindsey and Meagan—I love you.
—CRAIG

To the Neb—thanks for taking this dangerous journey with such courage.
And to Craig—indeed you have.
—JOHN

CONTENTS

ACKNOWLEDGMENTS

Thanks again to Jenny, Kyle, Brian, Sealy, and Mike.

The Journey of

DESIRE

Journal & Guidebook

INTRODUCTION

You are about to embark on what may be the most life-changing journey you've ever taken. This is not a simple workbook you're about to do. This is not a quick run down to the market for a gallon of milk and a loaf of bread. This is a mission on the level of the *Illiad* or *Pilgrim's Progress* or *The Lord of the Rings*—a desperate quest through dangerous country to a destination that is, beyond all your wildest hopes, indescribably good. The more you are able to think about what you are doing in more heroic and mythical terms, the better it will go for you.

Knowing quite well that this is no stroll in the park you are about to undertake, we'd like to offer a bit of counsel before you set out. The first piece of advice is about the nature of a *journey*. Ulysses sailed; Pilgrim and Frodo walked the better part of their quests. We postmoderns haven't anything in our experience to equal that. Thanks to modern air travel (the way most people take their adventures these days), we think nothing of hopping over thousands of miles of terrain in a matter of moments. I think it's bred a sort of impatience with any journey we now take. We're quite put out if we're delayed by a few hours from accomplishing what would have taken our ancestors *months* to get through.

And that impatience is a dangerous thing when it comes to *interior* journeys, spiritual quests, pilgrimages of the soul. For in these journeys we must cover the miles step-by-step, feeling the terrain as we pass through it, responding to its challenges. There is no rushing this; there are no shortcuts. But that is what makes it so beautiful and dangerous and wonderful. We don't snap a few photos and rush on; rather, *we are changed* by our travels. I think C. H. Spurgeon had this in mind when he warned that a pilgrim will be better served "by one book thoroughly mastered than by twenty books he has merely skimmed. Little learning and much pride come of hasty reading." Or hasty travel, we might add.

In other words, take your time. Beginning to understand your heart, to hear its pulse, to know its desires and passions, is perhaps the most important skill to learn, yet the most difficult as well. For many of you, life has done your heart much damage, numbing you and leaving you almost deaf to your heart's whispers. Be patient . . . it will come. Approach this as a quest for an elusive treasure you must take on foot. That sort of mindset will serve you well.

And now for a few thoughts on the nature of desire. Your desires will seem, at most times, a secret that may surface and then hide again in the deeper places of your heart. Recalling these defining desires cannot be rushed, or, for that matter, orchestrated. It takes time, reflection, and allowing your heart to be moved as you sort through things. Throughout this journey a recurring exercise will involve *remembering* and *articulating*—remembering more and further clarifying your own desires. Sometimes it will help to recall certain music, movies, books, friends, adventures, or photos that stirred your soul.

This uncovering of desire is *personal* and *unique*. Go to the places that will stir your memories of your desires, yearnings for life, your hopes and aspirations. Would looking through a photo album or some old videos do it? Perhaps recalling and listening to your favorite music from the past (what made it your favorite?), returning to your old neighborhood, or a special location (a park, cabin, store) might help. You'll notice that we've responded to a number of the questions with our own journaling. I take one chapter, Craig takes another, and so on through the journal. We did so partly because writing this evoked so much within our own hearts, and partly because we hope it will be helpful to you. Sometimes hearing the inner thoughts of someone else can help you identify your own. But that's all those entries are there for; please don't let them limit the nature of your response in any way. After all, this is *your* journey.

Some of the questions we've posed might seem repetitious from chapter to chapter. There's a reason for that. This is a journey of discovery and exploration, and as you move forward you'll come to new and deeper insights. Allow yourself to revisit issues when we bring them up again—you might be surprised what more you learn.

One more thing about desire: it will help you greatly to begin to distinguish your *desires* from the *objects* that seem to have aroused them, or promise to fulfill them. What God uses to awaken our desire is not always what he brings to us in order to complete it. This is not a bait-and-switch game played by a cheap magician; it is simply that God always works with us wherever we are, while ever desiring to lead us "further up and further in." C. S Lewis used the marvelous illustration of two children overhearing their parents discussing the delicious joys of sex. Having no experience or maturity for that sort of thing, the children concluded that the grown-ups must be talking about chocolate. Let your desire be awakened by all that has ever roused it, but do not insist on writing the end of this journey too quickly or too narrowly. As G. K. Chesterton reminds us, one of the essential ingredients of joy is the element of surprise.

INSPIRATION

At the outset of each chapter, or "mile" of the journey, we've recommended a song or a movie that we've found to help us (and many others) in our own journeys. You might want to listen to the song or watch the movie before setting out, or somewhere along that mile. Of course, you'll have your own inspirations that have meant something to you as well—by all means, use them. And keep an eye out for those gifts of inspiration God will bring during your travels; it will be a delightful surprise to watch what he offers at each stage of your voyage. Annie Dillard says, "The world is fairly studded and strewn with unwrapped gifts and free surprises . . . cast broadside from a generous hand."

Above all else, you must remember: you are not taking this journey alone. Jesus promised, "Unless I go away, the Counselor will not come to you; but if I go, I will send him to you . . . He will guide you into all truth" (John 16:7, 13 NIV). You have a Guide for this journey, and he is far more committed to your success than you are yourself. Thank God for that.

> May the road rise to meet you
> May the wind be always at your back
> And may the Lord hold you in the hollow of his hand.

—JOHN AND CRAIG

OUR HEART'S DEEPEST SECRET

> It seems to me we can never give up longing and wishing
> while we are alive. There are certain things we feel to be
> beautiful and good, and we must hunger for them.
> —GEORGE ELIOT

> But I still haven't found what I'm looking for.
> —U2

⸺ Counsel for the Journey

As you set out on the first leg of your journey, it might be good to remember what it was like to begin the first day of exercise, or a new job, or the next grade level at school in the fall. It felt a little awkward at first, didn't it? It took time to find your stride. This journal will probably feel the same way. Remember—our desires often seem a secret that may surface at times and then hide again in the deeper places of our heart. Recalling these defining desires cannot be rushed, or for that matter, orchestrated. It takes time, reflection, and allowing your heart to be moved as you sort through things.

In this chapter, what you're after is to awaken the deep desires of your heart and begin to put some words to it all. That's about it. The exercises are designed to arouse your desires, bring them up from the places we all tend to bury them, and help you articulate them.

⸺ Inspiration

There is a classic song by the band U2 called "I Still Haven't Found What I'm Looking For," which presents the yearning of our hearts through simple though passionate lyrics and soaring choruses. (How much of the music you love presents this theme of desire for something not yet embraced?) I (John—I'll be writing this first chapter) love the live version, complete with gospel choir, off the *Rattle and Hum* CD. Listen to this as loud as you can and see if your heart goes in the same direction as mine: *Lord, I do, I really do desire more. More of Life. More of you.*

*O*nce upon a time there lived a sea lion who had lost the sea.

He lived in a country known as the barren lands. High on a plateau, far from any coast, it was a place so dry and dusty that it could only be called a desert. A kind of coarse grass grew in patches here and there, and a few trees were scattered across the horizon. But mostly, it was dust. And sometimes wind, which together make one very thirsty. Of course, it must seem strange to you that such a beautiful creature should wind up in a desert at all. He was, mind you, a sea lion. But things like this do happen.

How the sea lion came to the barren lands, no one could remember. It all seemed so very long ago. So long, in fact, it appeared as though he had always been there. Not that he belonged in such an arid place. How could that be? He was, after all, a sea lion. But as you know, once you have lived so long in a certain spot, no matter how odd, you come to think of it as home.

Take a moment and respond to this opening passage from the story of the sea lion. What thoughts or feelings does it evoke in you? Is there anything about your own life over the years that resonates with the sea lion's plight?

SETTING FORTH

There is a secret set within each of our hearts. It often goes unnoticed, we rarely can put words to it, and yet it guides us throughout the days of our lives. This secret remains hidden for the most part in our deepest selves. It is simply the desire for life as it was meant to be . . . It is elusive, to be sure. It seems to come and go at will . . . And though it seems to taunt us, and may at times cause us great pain, we know when it returns that it is priceless. For if we could recover this desire, unearth it from beneath all other distractions, and embrace it as our deepest treasure, we would discover the secret of our existence. (pp. 1–2)

Your existence has a deep meaning. Yet for most of us, it remains hidden, shrouded, buried beneath all the other pressures and demands and busyness of life. But it doesn't go away. Your life has a secret, something written deep in your heart. Have you ever stopped to wonder, *What is the point of my life? Who am I, really? Why am I even here—why did God create me?* How would you respond to those questions now? What is the secret of your life?

Several years ago I (John) would have answered, "All I know is, there's got to be more. I don't know what it is yet, but I know that the life I'm living can't be the fulfillment of my destiny." More recently, though, I think I could say some things that are deeply true about the secret of my life. I know I'm here to set hearts free. A William Wilberforce to free the hearts of men and women. (God spoke that to me through a book several years ago). I know I'm meant to write and speak about the heart and lead a fellowship. I know I need wilderness, that my heart is wild and free. I know the life I've chosen, the friends I have, the way my family lives is deeply true—truer than it's ever been. I'm living in a MUCH larger story. And I'm deeply grateful that I'm able to say that because there were many, many years of just feeling . . . lost.

Isn't there a life you have been searching for all your days? You may not always be aware of your search, and there are times when you seem to have abandoned looking altogether. But again and again it returns to us, this yearning that cries out for the life we prize . . . You see, even while we are doing other things, "getting on with life," we still have an eye out for the life we secretly want. When someone seems to have gotten it together we wonder, *How did he do it?* Maybe if we read the same book, spent time with him, went to his church, things would come together for us as well. You see, we can never entirely give up our quest. (pp. 1, 11)

If your life could be better this next year, what would it look like? What would change?

Is there anything about someone else's life that really looks good to you right now?

WHISPERS OF JOY

The clue as to who we really are and why we are here comes to us through our heart's desire. But it comes in surprising ways, and so often goes unnoticed, or misunderstood. Once in a while life comes together for us in a way that feels so good and right and what we've been waiting for. These are the moments in our lives that we wish could go on forever. They aren't necessarily the "Kodak moments," weddings and births and great achievements. More often than not they come in subtler, unexpected ways, as if to sneak up on us.

Think of times in your life that made you wish for all the world that you had the power to make time stand still. Are they not moments of love, moments of joy? Simple moments of rest and quiet when all seems to be well. Something in your heart says, *Finally—it has come. This is what I was made for!* (pp. 2–3)

Unearthing our desire isn't a quick and easy thing. So start with just a good moment from the last few weeks—something that may seem rather simple, but it made you glad. What happened? Why was it a good moment?

OK, we're getting warmed up. Now think of *another* good moment from the past year. What happened? Why was it a good moment?

Now pick one of the *best* moments from the past few years. Write about it, as I wrote about the evening my family shared in the Tetons. (In fact, it might help to reread that passage from pages 3–4 before you write your own account.) Who was there with you? What were your surroundings? *Why* was it such a good moment? If you have a photo from that time, it might help to look at it as you write.

Tracks of a Fellow Traveler

One of my best moments came at the end of a wonderful day. My family and a group of our friends had all gone camping together for a week. The last day was spent at a high mountain lake; canoeing, swimming, playing, hiking, a beautiful warm day . . . At dusk, sun-tired and happy, we decided to eat at the barbecue offered at the lodge. Easy and good food! There was a musician playing at the barbecue–quite good, singing and playing country songs on his guitar. My golden moment came about halfway through the meal, when we were all seated at three tables clustered together and we had wooed the musician over to us. Someone requested James Taylor's "Carolina," and he sang it well. We all knew the chorus and joined in singing, our voices blending as our lives had blended over the past week and months. Even the children sang. And I had such a feeling of togetherness, of belonging, of a shared past and a shared future . . . hope, beauty, adventure, harmony . . . lovely. (Stasi)

As the old Scottish poet George MacDonald knew so well, *something is calling to us* in moments like these.

> Yet hints come to me from the realm unknown;
> Airs drift across the twilight border land,
> Odored with life;
> . . . whispers to my heart are blown
> That fill me with a joy I cannot speak,
> Yea, from whose shadow words drop faint and weak. *(Diary of an Old Soul)* (p. 4)

What was calling to you through your memory that you just wrote about? For me and for Stasi, it was a sense of intimacy and belonging, of beauty and adventure that made our hearts say, *This is how I was meant to live.* What was it for you?

Now think about other "hints" that come to you. What are the movies and music, the people, events, and places that have really stirred your heart over the past few years? Just name them here.

Lord, there are so many. Where to begin? Wilderness—deep, rugged, forbidding wilderness. Kissing Stasi. The desert in Moab. Rachmaninoff's Adagio from Symphony no 2. Windy nights at Ute Park. Last night's dinner with Lynn. The last fifteen minutes of Braveheart. The sound track that goes with it. Wow . . . this could go on for a long time. Christmas Eve. Horses. Ranches. Western art. The last day at Lost Valley. The photo on my bookcase of Brent and me. Gladiator. The Last of the Mohicans. Snowshoeing up by the Tyndall glacier. I'd better stop and let you write.

ECHOES FROM THE PAST

Sometimes these moments go unrecognized as they unfold, but their secret comes to us years later in our longing to relive them. Aren't there times in your life that, if you could, you would love to return to? I grew up in Los Angeles but spent my boyhood summers in Oregon where both my mother's and my father's parents lived. There was a beauty and innocence and excitement to those days. Woods to explore, rivers to fish, grandparents to fuss over me. My parents were young and in love, and the days were full of adventures I did not have to create or pay for, but only live in and enjoy. Rafting and swimming in the Rogue River. Playing in the park. Huckleberry pie at Becky's along the road to Crater Lake. We all have places in our pasts when life, if only for a moment, seemed to be coming together in the way we knew in our hearts it was always meant to be. (p. 5)

Is there a time and place in your life that you would love to return to? When was it—and why would you love to relive it again, if only for a day? (It might be good to look through some old photo albums and remember some of the "firsts" of your life.)

People tend to handle the past in one of two extremes. Either they try to push it all away, "put it behind them" and never speak of it again, or they might yearn and feel nostalgic and talk as though life will never be that good again. Which do you tend toward? Why?

Much of my life has been good...and much of it has also been painful. I see now that I'm one of those people who just want to get past it all. I actually looked forward to growing up, growing older, so I could put the past behind me. I rarely look at old photo albums, rarely think about the past. I've never organized a family reunion. I'm hardly ever nostalgic. I focus on the future, whats ahead. I think I'm beginning to better understand why. Thinking about the past rouses longing and hope and pain that I'd just rather not deal with . . . that is, until I realize "I want my whole heart back!"

SHOUTS OF LAMENT

Now for the more difficult side of desire. It's hard for most of us to talk about our losses. But the secret of our hearts is also coming to us even in our greatest losses. So again, let's start with something simpler and more current—a bad day you've had recently (and given the way life tends to go in a fallen world, I think it's safe to ask about recently). What happened? *Why* was it a bad day? And what were you tempted to conclude about life in that moment?

What has been one of the biggest hassles of the last few years? What would have brought you relief ?

Now, this is going to be harder, but hang in there with me. What has been one of your greatest losses or disappointments? Whom or what did you lose, and what did the thing you lost mean to you?

Is there anyone or anything that you wish could be restored to you?

Simone Weil was right; there are only two things that pierce the human heart: beauty and affliction. Moments we wish would last forever and moments we wish had never begun. What are we to make of these messengers? How are we to interpret what they are saying? (p. 8)

What *have* you done with the way your life has unfolded? I mean, how have you made sense of it all? Put those two events together, the joys and the losses you just wrote about. What does your heart do with it all?

I hunker down, that's what I do. I want the joy, for sure. But I fear the hurt and heartache I know is coming. So I think what I do is sort of hunker down, and try to grab at little pleasures as I can while guarding against major disappointments. I feel like a turtle, ready to pull my head into my shell at any moment.

THE SAME OLD THING

Something awful has happened; something terrible. Something worse, even, than the fall of man. For in that greatest of all tragedies, we merely lost Paradise—and with it, everything that made life worth living. What has happened since is unthinkable: we've gotten used to it. We're broken in to the idea that this is just the way things are. The people who walk in great darkness have adjusted their eyes. Regardless of our religious or philosophical beliefs, most of us live as though this life is pretty much the way things are supposed to be. (p. 9)

You may not be aware how used to it you've really gotten. That's a symptom of learning to live with life in a fallen world. We simply, slowly adjust. But consider it this way: Do you have big dreams for yourself? Name five. And if you don't have big dreams for yourself, what might that say about how you "hunker down"?

Think with me for a moment. How has life turned out differently from the way you thought it would? If you are single, did you want to be? If you are married, is this the marriage you hoped for? Do you long to have children, or in having them, are you delighted with the course they've chosen for their lives? Your friendships—are they as rich and deep and lasting as you want? When the holidays roll around, do you look forward with eager anticipation to the time you'll spend with the people in your life? And afterward, as you pack away the decorations and clean up the mess, did the reality match your expectations?

How about your work, your place in the world—do you go to bed each night with a deep sense of having made a lasting contribution? Do you enjoy ongoing recognition for your unique successes? Are you even working in a field that fits you? Are you working at all? (p. 10)

How *has* life turned out differently from the way you thought it would, or at least kinda hoped it would? If your answer is not easy and immediate, use the questions I asked in the passage above to think about the key areas of your life.

Tracks of a Fellow Traveler

She was going to be an actress and I was going to learn to fly
She took off to find the footlights, I took off for the sky . . .
And here she is acting happy inside her handsome home
And me I'm flying in my taxi, taking tips and getting stoned.
("Taxi" by Harry Chapin, © copyright 1996, 1997, 1998, 1999, 2000, 2001 The Harry Chapin Archive)

What do you see God doing in and for others that you so wish he would do for *you*?

Now, what if I told you that this is how it will always be, that this life as you now experience it will go on forever just as it is, without improvement of any kind? Your health will stay as it is; your finances will remain as they are, your relationships, your work, all of it. (p. 10)

React to that with as much honesty as you can muster.

IN DEFENSE OF DISCONTENT

By the grace of God, we cannot quite pull it off. In the quiet moments of the day we sense a nagging within, a discontentment, a hunger for something else. But because we have not solved the riddle of our existence, we assume that something is wrong—not with life, but with us. *Everyone else seems to be getting on with things. What's wrong with me?* We feel guilty about our chronic disappointment. *Why can't I just learn to be happier in my job, in my marriage, in my church, in my group of friends?* (pp. 10–11)

Have you ever felt that—that something is wrong with you, that if you did things better, if *you* were better, life wouldn't have turned out this way? Do you feel a twinge of guilt about wanting a different life?

Oh yeah. Nobody in my extended family lives from desire. So few people in my old church did I finally stopped going. I did not fit in. The accuser is always on my case, telling me how wrong I am for this desire or that one.

We are desire. It is the essence of the human soul, the secret of our existence. Absolutely nothing of human greatness is ever accomplished without it. Not a symphony has been written, a mountain climbed, an injustice fought, or a love sustained apart from desire. (p. 11)

Whoa. Have you ever thought that you *are* desire? And that desire is a really good and noble thing?

What did your parents teach you about your desires? Did they affirm them—or ridicule them? Did they live from desire?

And how about your friends—what do they do with desire?

What has been the message to you, from your world and your life, about desire?

Tracks of a Fellow Traveler

This is what the LORD Almighty says: "I am very jealous for Zion; I am burning with jealousy for her." (Zech. 8:2 NIV)

O Jerusalem, Jerusalem . . . how often I have longed to gather your children together, as a hen gathers her chicks under her wings, but you were not willing. (Matt. 23:37 NIV)

I have eagerly desired to eat this Passover with you before I suffer. (Luke 22:15 NIV)

Jesus was a man of deep desire. It's the secret of his life. Hebrews says it's what sustained him in his darkest hour—that he endured the cross because he so deeply desired what was on the other side, what his sacrifice would accomplish (12:2).

The secret that begins to solve the riddle of our lives is simply this: we are the sea lion who lost the sea. Life as usual is not the life we truly want. It is not the life we truly need. It is not the life we were made for. If we would only listen to our hearts, to what G. K. Chesterton called our "divine discontent," we would learn the secret of our existence . . . "We have come to the wrong star . . . That is what makes life at once so splendid and so strange. The true happiness is that we *don't* fit. We come from somewhere else. We have lost our way." (pp. 11–12)

Now let this sink in: you are the sea lion who lost the sea. *You* are the sea lion who lost the sea. Does it begin to make sense of things? You were made to live in Paradise. Let that sink in for a moment. Put the book down and repeat it to yourself five times: *I was made to live in Paradise.* What does your heart do with that truth?

Wow . . . I'm surprised at my response. I'm angry, but my editor won't print what I really want to say. Why couldn't we have just obeyed? Why did we have to throw it all away? I want to weep. God, can we ever get it back? Really? Is it really true, this vague promise of a real life that is coming? Help me to believe it.

Pascal says that the troubles and woes and heartaches of our lives prove that we are as a king who lost his country, a "dethroned monarch." Of course that fits with the biblical record, which tells us that our original position was to be God's regents, his governors over a fabulously beautiful and wonderful creation (read Genesis 1–2). Now let me ask,

Should the king in exile pretend he is happy there? Should he not seek his own country? His miseries are his ally; they urge him on. Let them grow, if need be. But do not forsake the secret of life; do not despise those kingly desires. We abandon he most important journey of our lives when we abandon desire. We leave our hearts by the side of the road and head off in the direction of fitting in, getting by, being productive, what have you . . . If you will look around, you will see that most people have abandoned the journey. They have lost heart. They are camped in places of resignation or indulgence, or trapped in prisons of despair. (pp. 13, 15)

How many people in your life does that describe—fitting in, getting by, resigned, just trying to live from day to day? Wait, let me ask it the other way: Can you name anyone in your life that *doesn't* describe?

TAKING UP THE QUEST

Bringing our heart along in our life's journey is the most important mission of our lives—and the hardest. It all turns on what we do with our desire. (pp. 14–15)

This statement is going to become a whole lot more clear as we go on. But let me try to explain it a little right here. Proverbs urges us to guard our hearts as if they were our most precious treasure, because it is "the wellspring of life" inside us (4:23 NIV). Among other things, your heart is the place where your deepest desires come from ("Delight yourself in the LORD and he will give you the desires *of your heart*" [Ps. 37:4 NIV, emphasis added]). So the way you handle desire is in fact the way you handle your heart. How have you handled desire in the past?

Striving and indulging—that's how I handled desire for years. Grasping for what I could arrange, denying those desires I couldn't take care of, vacillating from just working hard and using busyness to keep myself from facing my heart to looking for a little something on the side. I have mishandled my desire for years.

We must return to the journey. Wherever we are, whatever we are doing, we must pick up the trail and follow the map that we have at hand. (p. 13)

Of course, you have taken up the journey. That's why you're going through this journal. What are you hoping to find?

Do you have any fears about this journey?

And in spite of those fears, how badly do you want to find the life you were *meant* to live?

Write out your prayer to God for this journey you are now embarking on.

Tracks of a Fellow Traveler

But I still haven't found
What I'm looking for.
But I still haven't found
What I'm looking for. . .
("I Still Haven't Found What I'm Looking For" by Bono, U2 © 1987 U2)

THE DILEMMA OF DESIRE

I never knew the dusk could break my heart
So much longing folding in
I'd give years away to have you here
To know I can't lose you again.
—FERNANDO ORTEGA

Who needs a heart when a heart can be broken?
—TINA TURNER

— Counsel for the Journey

If it was easy, everybody would be living from desire. We know it isn't going to be easy, either, to really know what it is we desire or to begin to actually live from our heart's desire. There is a fear, a check, a hesitation deep inside all of us. As John ended the last chapter:

Bringing our heart along in our life's journey is the most important mission of our lives—and the hardest . . . Life provides any number of reasons and occasions to abandon desire. Certainly, one of the primary reasons is that it creates for us our deepest dilemmas. To desire something and not to have it—is this not the source of nearly all our pain and sorrow?

In order to move forward, you cannot just pretend that deep hesitation is not there. You must bring up from the depths of your heart your deep ambivalence about desire—and the specific reasons why.

— Inspiration

A song I'd (Craig here—this is my chapter) like to recommend comes from many years back, which in simple, beautiful ways depicts the choices of one man hurt by love, never to love again. It's "I am a Rock," by Paul Simon and Art Garfunkel. His commitment to build a safe and sheltered life is so true of all of us. I like the version on *The Best of Simon and Garfunkel* CD.

There was a time, many years back, when the sea lion knew he was lost. In those days, he would stop every traveler he met to see if they might help him find his way back to the sea.

But no one seemed to know the way.

On he searched, but never finding. After years without success, the sea lion took refuge beneath a solitary tree beside a very small water hole. The tree provided refuge from the burning rays of the sun, which was very fierce in that place. And the water hole, though small and muddy, was wet, in its own way. Here he settled down and got on as best he could.

I think we all, in some past time, in some fashion, have tried to find our way to the life we desire. We leaned upon others but no one seemed to know the way. Like the sea lion, we, too, after years without success, eventually settle down beside a small, muddy water hole. It's there we get on as best we can, taking refuge from what seems like a cruel desire for the sea.

What small story, what water hole, have you settled into in order to just get on with life? Where does your sense of security come from these days (what do you find yourself worrying about)? And where do you go for a little pleasure (what do you find yourself daydreaming about)?

SETTING FORTH

Desire is the source of our most noble aspirations and our deepest sorrows. The pleasure and the pain go together; indeed, they emanate from the same region in our hearts. We cannot live without the yearning, and yet the yearning sets us up for disappointment—sometimes deep and devastating disappointment. (p. 19)

The account of the 1996 Everest disaster is a haunting story of the unwavering intensity of desire. Should they not have tried? Many have said they were foolish even to begin. Do we reach for nothing in life because our reaching opens us up to tragedy? What's been your philosophy—maybe even your advice to others—on that question? Have you urged others to follow *their* dreams? Why . . . or why not?

FRIEND OR FOE?

Tina Turner may have captured a governing passion of our lives in her lyric "Who needs a heart when a heart can be broken?" To continue the journey of desire makes us vulnerable to a deeper ongoing pain than we may be willing to endure. Desire begins to feel like our worst enemy. What desires in your life are feeling like enemies these days—because of the pain they bring or the trouble they get you into?

Fantine, one of the tragic characters in Victor Hugo's novel *Les Misérables* . . . remembers being young and unafraid, that time in our lives when dreams are "made and used and wasted." She tells of a love that came to her, filling her days with endless wonder. He became the father of her child and then, one day, disappeared. She dreams he will return, but knows he never will.

> *I had a dream in time gone by*
> *When hope was high*
> *And life worth living*
> *I dreamed that love would never die*
> *I dreamed that God would be forgiving*
>
> *I had a dream my life would be*
> *So different from this hell I'm living*
> *So different now from what it seemed*
> *Now life has killed the dream I dreamed.* (pp. 20–21)

Can you remember the dreams or desires you had as a child for your life? What did you "once upon a time" think you would become? This question may require leisurely looking through old photos/videos, or perhaps inquiring of parents or family members, "What did you think I would end up being/doing?"

Can I (Craig) even remember the desires and dreams I once had, but now are seemingly lost? As I go through the photos of my childhood, I do remember . . . trips, adventures, games, reading stories and biographies of the great and good among us. What was once called "pretend" I now understand as yearning as I set myself into the stories of others. Courageous missions of WWII pilots, the adventures of the mountain men taming the West . . . I, too, would accomplish something heroic in my life. Maybe more then than now, I knew there was a reason for me to be here; I was no widget maker. Those grand desires captured me. But somewhere, somehow, they disappeared. Yet even as I recall those more-innocent times, there's something inside that seems awakened by the memories. Are they still there?

Yeah, it's embarrassing to say it, but it's true, the desire to be a part of something large, not in size but nobility, to be a part of something heroic is one desire that got lost. Another is to be part of a family in which we see one another's glory, smiling, laughing as we never have, receiving from one another a joy no other circle of people could ever provide. Dear Lord, may it be.

WHEN DREAMS DIE

I am not alone in this. Most of you will by this time have lost a parent, a spouse, even a child. Your hopes for your career have not panned out. Your health has given way. Relationships have turned sour. We all know the dilemma of desire, how awful it feels to open our hearts to joy, only to have grief come in. They go together. We know that. What we don't know is what to do with it, how to live in this world with desire so deep in us and disappointment lurking behind every corner. After we've taken a few arrows, dare we even desire? (p. 23)

John shares about the death of Brent (pp. 6–8, 21–22). What words can truly describe the loss of one's closest friend, shared dreams . . . and what feels like life itself? Wouldn't we all understand the "shutting down" of desire in such a situation; wouldn't we compassionately allow and even encourage someone in such pain to bury their desire and get on as best they could?

Allow me to ask a question we would do well to consider again and again. What dreams have you had that have seemingly died along the way?

But have they really, totally died? Beneath the ashes of loss, pain, the wasted years and distractions, might there still be a few coals of burning desire? The desire for something more . . . much more? Are you willing to let them rise and then to embrace them? What do you fear?

I have come to the point that I am able to start looking at ranches again, but I can barely open myself to friendship. Still, something in me knows that to kill desire is to kill my heart altogether. As Langston Hughes wrote,

> *Hold fast to dreams,*
> *For if dreams die*
> *Life is a broken-winged bird*
> *That cannot fly.*
> *Hold fast to dreams,*
> *For if dreams go,*
> *Life is a barren field*
> *Frozen with snow.* ("Dreams")

Do we form no friendships because our friends might be taken from us? Do we refuse to love because we may be hurt? Do we forsake our dreams because hope has been deferred? To desire is to open our hearts to the possibility of pain; to shut down our hearts is to die altogether. For the full proverb reads this way: "Hope deferred makes the heart sick, *but when dreams come true, there is life and joy*" (13:12 NLT, emphasis added). The road to life and joy lies through, not around, the heartsickness of hope deferred. A good friend came to this realization recently. As we sat talking over breakfast, he put words to our dilemma:

I stand at the crossroads, and I am afraid of the desire. For forty-one years I've tried to control my life by killing the desire, but I can't. Now I know it. But to allow it to be, to let it out, is frightening because I know I'll have to give up control of my life. Is there another option?

The option most of us have chosen is to reduce our desire to a more manageable size. We allow it out only in small doses—just what we can arrange for. Dinner out, a new sofa, a vacation to look forward to, a little too much to drink. It's not working. (pp. 23–24)

So, how well, really, have you done arranging for some satisfaction of your desires at those muddy water holes you identified at the beginning of this section? Is this the abundant life you are living?

I've lingered at so many muddy water holes in my journey. Running, food, the praise of people, competency, a "buzz," being "the life of the party," didn't satisfy but seemed to moisten my lips. Hiding, distractions, playing it safe, sex, appearing more righteous than I really was, coming across as passionately authentic, "real," living in shame, have provided meager, but nonetheless some bit of shade.

I so very deeply, still, yearn to be involved in something large, meaningful, pioneering, wild, worthy. Yet it seems so much of my life is a small story better described as respected, spiritual, secure . . . safe . . . Deep inside, I sense the desire to climb some mountain . . . but I haven't yet. Ah, but I want to. Lord help me.

Like the sea lion, we do settle down and lose desire, but it's rarely a conscious decision; it's more subtle. In fact, the justification makes sense. From within or through others we accept the advice: "Lower your expectations and you'll not be disappointed," or "Your desires are unrealistic," or the dismissing label, "You're a dreamer, a romantic idealist." What has led you to reduce life to getting on as best you can?

Though I am aware of my heart whispering desires for a life that's much "more" engaging, it seems like the "other" voices are louder, more persuasive, influential. Those voices that say, "It's not true . . . not for you," "You don't have what it takes . . . it'll never happen," "You're a dreamer." And because, in many ways, past hopes, desires, and efforts have failed or fallen short, it feels safer to hang on to some dreams, enough to stay "alive," but never risk pursuing them. And somewhere along the line I've come to believe that some desires/dreams are meant to be kept hidden away in storage, never pursued, never lost. Kinda like my home emergency supplies that "I'm not supposed to get into" unless I absolutely have to.

Oh, free me from the paralysis of fear, of past disappointment, God. Please wake, stir up, and free the desires of my heart that I, too, might be thrust into the pursuit of that for which I've been made and have always desired to be and do. I long to have desire that would overcome any obstacle and count no sacrifice as too great.

Let me invite you to write out a prayer or a piece of poetry, prose, or even a song to God that expresses your heart at this moment and point in your journey.

THE BATTLE BETWEEN US

Unrealized, unfulfilled desire has an immense power to shape our lives and relationships. Those things that plague our hearts and souls will have an impact on those around us.

> The life we have is so far from the life we truly want, and it doesn't take us long to find someone to blame. In order for our longings to be filled, we need the cooperation of others. I long for a loving embrace and a kind word when I get home. I long for my boys to listen attentively when I talk about important life lessons. I want my work to be appreciated. I want my friends to be there for me in hard times. "No man is an island," wrote John Donne, and he could have been speaking of desire. We need others—it's part of our design. Very few of our desires are self-fulfilling; *all* our deepest longings require others to come through for us. Inevitably, someone stands in the way. (pp. 25–26)

Can you see this dynamic of frustrated desire at work in some of your fractured relationships? Who hasn't come through for you, and how have you battled them as a result? Write down a couple of disappointing or fractured relationships here—and then see if you can put some words to the specific issues lying beneath. Who blocked whose desire?

Just yesterday I "put it together." My recent sleeplessness and "agitation" (it couldn't be anger or rage could it?) with just about everyone I work and live with is, once again, pretty easily understood. I insist those around me cooperate in making life unfold according to my script, which in its most recent edition goes something like this: "Craig, with incredible insight, strength, courage, and compassion (a model of righteousness), empties himself in sacrificial service to a church on the brink of disaster. With his only desire being the church's return to its first love and the glory of God, he is victorious in heroically reviving the pastor's and elders' passions, redirecting their ministries. The congregation, in jubilant celebration, acknowledge my unique anointing with shouts of praise only the apostle Paul would be familiar with." Oh God, I cry as I laugh at the shallow desires I've lived in recently. Lord, forgive me for the little mud hole I chose to live in, and for the anger, hatred, aloofness, and arrogance others have surely seen and felt from me.

At its best, the world is indifferent to my desires. The air traffic controllers aren't the least affected when I've been traveling for a week and the plane they've chosen to cancel is my last chance to get home to my family. So long as it doesn't affect them, they couldn't care less. We suffer the violation of indifference on a daily basis, from friends, from family, from complete strangers. We think we've grown to accept it as part of life, but the effect is building inside us. We weren't made to be ignored. And though we try to pretend it doesn't really matter, the collective effect of living in a world apathetic to our existence is doing damage to our souls. Events such as bad traffic or delayed flights are merely the *occasions* for our true desperation to come out. As our desires come into direct conflict with the desires of another person, things get downright hostile. (p. 26)

Dan Allender points out, . . . "Our desires—from picking the quickest line at the bank to the overwhelming hope that our children will walk righteously with the Lord—are rarely satisfied in a way that relieves the ache of incompleteness . . . Our heart seems to rage against the ache. Our typical response to the heartbreak and sorrow of disappointment is murderous rage . . . We want someone to pay." (*Bold Love*) (p. 25)

OK—who has really made you mad lately? What desire of yours have they thwarted, blocked, ignored?

I really appreciate the honesty of Gerald May when he says,

Choosing love will open spaces of immense beauty and joy for you, but you will be hurt. You already know this. You have retreated from love countless times in your life because of it. We all have. We have been and will be hurt by the loss of loved ones, by what they have done to us and we to them. Even in the bliss of love there is a certain exquisite pain: the pain of too much beauty, of overwhelming magnificence. Further, no matter how perfect a love may be, it is never really satisfied . . . In both joy and pain, love is boundless. (*The Awakened Heart*) (p. 19)

Name the people who have hurt you in your life. How and why did they hurt you?

How have those hurts shaped your approach to living and loving? Can you see that? Are you more cautious now, more guarded—maybe even totally fortressed?

Tracks of a Fellow Traveler

Don't talk of love;
well, I've heard the word before;
it's sleeping in my memory.
I won't disturb the slumber
of feelings that have died.
If I never loved
I never would have cried.
("I Am a Rock" by Paul Simon" 1965)

The Beast Within

There is a reason Jesus chose lust and murder as examples of what happens when desire goes mad within us. He knew what our desperate hearts naturally do when our desires come into conflict. He knew to what lengths we would go to seek satisfaction of our soul's hunger. For the battle of desire rages not only between us, but *within* us. (p. 28)

> Something has gone wrong deep within me and gets the better of me every time. It happens so regularly that it's predictable. The moment I decide to do good, sin is there to trip me up. I truly delight in God's commands, but it's pretty obvious that not all of me joins in that delight. Parts of me covertly rebel, and just when I least expect it, they take charge. (Rom. 7:20–23 *The Message*)

> For the sinful nature desires what is contrary to the Spirit, and the Spirit what is contrary to the sinful nature. They are in conflict with each other, so that you do not do what you want. (Gal. 5:17 NIV)

This battle within is between two clusters of desires with very different origins. On the one hand, there are the desires of our new covenant heart that are in concert with the Spirit (the desire to do "good"). In opposition to these are those desires contrary to the Spirit that are rooted in our sin nature. Can you identify and begin to recognize these very different desires in your day-to-day living? Describe a recent battle within.

My wife and I were invited to dinner with a couple I simply do not enjoy being with. One set of desires felt strong and went something like this: "Don't go . . . They are 'drainers,' having nothing to offer . . . Are you kidding me? There's nothing in me that wants to spend three boring, miserably superficial hours in conversational cul-de-sacs. I'm not going." The opposing desire, which is easily missed if living on autopilot, seems deeper and truer to who I am and went like this: "I long to touch people's lives and hearts like Christ. This couple, with all their rough quirky edges, are reaching out to us for something. This is an opportunity God may be providing to spend time with them and be available for God to use me in their lives. I'd like to go."

And is there a pretty common "battle within," a regular argument you have in your mind, or a regular struggle you have to resist? What is going on there—do you know?

There is a nagging awareness inside us, warning that we'd better not feel our hunger too deeply or it will undo us. We might do something crazed, desperate. And so we are caught on the horns of a dilemma; our unmet desires are a source of trouble, and it feels as if it will get worse if we allow ourselves to feel how much we do desire. Not only that, we often don't even know what we desire . . . We try food, tennis, television, or sex, going from one thing to another, never quite finding satisfaction. The reason we don't know what we want is that we're so *unacquainted* with our desire. (pp. 29–30)

How acquainted are you with your heart's desire? Take a struggle you've been having with sin or temptation. What are you wanting? Why does it feel as if that object is the only way to get what you are wanting? Can you begin to separate your *desire* from the *object* you've been turning to?

Continuing with the theme of "unacquainted with desire," has your work in this journal been hard or easy up to this point? Can you make a list here of the things you are truly desiring at this season of your life? What is it you want?

And after you've made your list, which of those *won't* you pursue—and why not?

We try to keep a safe distance between our daily lives and our heart's desire because it causes us so much trouble. We're surprised by our anger and threatened by what feels like a ravenous bear within us. Do we really want to open Pandora's box? . . .

Dare we awaken our hearts to their true desires? Dare we come alive? Is it better, as the saying goes, to have loved and lost, than never to have loved at all? We're not so sure. After his divorce, a friend's father decided to remain single the rest of his life. As he told his son, "It's easier to stay out than to get out." Our dilemma is this: we can't seem to live with desire, and we can't live without it. (p. 30)

Be really honest now: What do you fear will happen if you live fully and freely from desire?

And what will happen to you—to your heart, your life—if you *don't* live from desire?

Tracks of a Fellow Traveler

I think it would be good to mention that sometimes there is a "waiting period" after a devastating loss before the heart is healed and open to a deep level of desire again. A fresh and present grief makes desire look like a fool. Who in their right mind would want to get up and do it all over again? But that's not what desire is demanding—it's simply saying, "Breathe again. Let beauty heal you . . . allow it passage. Notice joy sprouting here and there. God's tenderness and mercy will slowly unravel the ache—it is a much better route than attempting to tranquilize your heart in numbness, which won't work anyway. Simply receive the gentleness of God, and as your heart is restored, desire will naturally spring forth once again." (Jen)

Finish this leg of your journey by writing out your prayer to God for the road ahead.

MILE THREE

DARE WE DESIRE?

Longing is the heart's treasury.
—AUGUSTINE

What do you want?
—JESUS OF NAZARETH

— Counsel for the Journey

I (John) ended the last chapter in the book with these thoughts:

> Our dilemma is this: we can't seem to live with desire, and we can't live
> without it. In the face of this quandary most people decide to bury the
> whole question and put as much distance as they can between themselves
> and their desires. It is a logical and tragic act. The tragedy is increased
> tenfold when this suicide of soul is committed under the conviction that
> this is precisely what Christianity recommends. We have never been more
> mistaken. (p. 30)

How sad to think that the overwhelming majority of Christians have been
taught that desire is an enemy—maybe *the* enemy—to living a good Christian
life. But it's true. My guess is, you're among them. I am too. You won't find it
easy to travel very far toward desire if some of your deepest beliefs about
God are in conflict with your quest. So, in this leg of the journey, we're
encouraging you to take a deeper look at what God thinks of your desire,
what he says he wants—not *from* you, but *for* you. This could mean a pretty
radical reformation of your thoughts about God and the Christian life. (That's
a good thing, by the way.)

All that many of you need to launch into a whole new passionate life is simply . . . permission.

— Inspiration

OK, it's an old film by now, but there remains a powerful lesson in *Chariots of Fire*, the true story of Olympic rivals Eric Liddle and Harold Abrams. If you've never seen it, or if it's been years since you have, take time to watch it this week. I (John) think you'll be deeply impacted by the contrast of a man whose heart is killed by the law (Abrams) and a man so freed by the gospel of grace that he runs for the sheer pleasure of God. It's a story of duty pitted against desire.

Had you journeyed in those days through the barren lands, you might have seen the sea lion for yourself. Quite often in the evening, he would go and sit upon his favorite rock, a very large boulder, which lifted him off the burning sand and allowed him a view of the entire country.

There he would remain for hours into the night, silhouetted against the sky. And on the best nights, when the wind shifted to the east, a faint smell of salt air would come to him on the breeze. Then he would close his eyes and imagine himself once more at the sea. When he lay himself down to sleep, he would dream of a vast, deep ocean. Twisting and turning, diving and twirling, he would swim and swim and swim. When he woke, he thought he heard the sound of breakers.

The sea was calling to him.

What are the ways in which your heart's desire has been calling to you over the past several months . . . years, even? How has God been stirring, awakening desire in you? Are there places you've been going to get alone with your heart, listen to the call? Are there daydreams you've been having? Has anything made you stop for a moment, turn and "listen" to a desire within—a song, something in a magazine, an event in someone else's life?

It's come back to horses, and a ranch. For years I've (John) walked away from that part of my heart, and that season in my life when as a boy-becoming-a-man I found my heart in the ranch life of my grandfather's cattle ranch. I picked up a magazine of Western art a few weeks ago, and God spoke—he took me back to some of my deepest desires, something beyond words set deep in my heart. Those paintings of cowboys and horses and mountains just about undid me.

SETTING FORTH

Now consider the crippled man at the pool of Bethesda. His story was chosen over thousands of others to be included in the New Testament, and I believe that part of the reason why is that it's *our* story too. You know him better than you might think.

> Think of the fellow on the ground for a moment; put yourself, literally, in his shoes. His entire life has been shaped by his brokenness. All his days he has wanted one thing. Forget riches. Forget fame. Life for this man was captured in one simple, unreachable desire. When the other children ran and played, he sat and watched. When his family stood at the temple to pray, he lay on the ground. Every time he needed to have a drink or to go to the bathroom, someone had to pick him up and take him there. (pp. 34–35)

Can you relate to the idea of "one simple, unreachable desire"? What has that been for you in the story of your life? It might be very current, or you may have to reach back a number of years to a time when you still wanted it. Can you name it?

At what point did he begin to lose hope? First a year, then two went by. Nothing, at least for him. Maybe someone else got a miracle; that would buy him some time. What about after five years with no results? Ten? How long can we sustain desire against continual disappointment? Some hold out longer than others, but eventually, we all move to a place of resignation or cynicism or bitterness. As the years rolled on, this man, like all of us, began to lose any vital heart connection to what he wanted . . . He had abandoned desire. (p. 35)

And what have *you* done with the core desires of your heart over the years? If someone got an honest look at how you've handled those deep desires, would they describe you at times as maybe a little resigned, or cynical . . . even bitter?

It's true. Even now, there are places I just don't want to go—desires I don't want to resurrect. Even though I'm looking, I'm having a hard time believing I will somehow have the ranch life again. And I know I've given up wanting a great relationship with my parents, I know that. They call me, but I don't really know what to say to them. Our conversations feel awkward, and I'm sorry for that. And I don't know how many times I've given up wanting more in my marriage because it just seems too hard to get there.

But I have noticed recently that when I push my heart away, when I shut down desire, almost immediately I want to go eat something, or buy something, or go find some adventure. God, help me stop going to resignation—no matter how painful that may be.

AN INVITATION TO DESIRE

This may come as a surprise to you: Christianity is not an invitation to become a moral person. It is not a program for getting us in line or for reforming society. It has a powerful effect upon our lives, but when transformation comes, it is always the *aftereffect* of something else, something at the level of our hearts. At its core, Christianity begins with an invitation to *desire*. (p. 35)

Does that come as a surprise to you? Was that what Christianity was explained to you to be—an invitation to desire? How do the "godly" people in your church handle desire?

Let's take a closer look at the way Jesus relates to people.

As he did with the fellow at the Sheep Gate, he is continually taking them into their hearts, to their deepest desires. The story of the two blind men on the road to Jericho repeats the theme. Jesus is passing by the spot where these two men have sat looking for a handout for who knows how long. They learn that Jesus is going by, and they cry out for him. Though the crowd tries to shut them up, they succeed in shouting over the ruckus and capturing the Master's attention. The parade stops. Jesus steps to the side of the road, and standing there before him are two men, nothing clearer than the fact that they are blind. "What do you want me to do for you?" Again the question. Again the obvious that must not be so obvious after all . . . Then there is the Samaritan woman whom Jesus meets at the well . . . What does he choose to talk to her about—her immorality? No, he speaks to her about her *thirst*. (pp. 35–36)

So here we have three stories—a paraplegic, two blind men, and a loose woman—and the theme is the same. Jesus asks them about their desire. Is *that* how you've understood Jesus' way with people? If Christ stood before you right now and could bring up something with you that he's wanted to talk to you about for sometime, what topic do you think he'd choose?

> Good grief—despite all my work on the subject, despite the fact that I do believe everything I've written here, I still have this nagging sense that what Jesus would really want to talk to me about is some failure of mine to live the way I'm supposed to—a lack of love, a loss of courage, or my small faith. It really stops me short—in a good way—to think that he'd talk to me about my thirst. It makes me . . . hopeful. Jesus, I'm a little nervous asking this (again), but I do invite you to come and talk to me, with me, about my heart. Talk to me about my desire. I want to go there with you.

Again and again and again, Jesus takes people back to their desires: "Ask and it will be given to you; seek and you will find; knock and the door will be opened to you" (Matt. 7:7 NIV). These are outrageous words, provocative words. *Ask, seek, knock*—these words invite and *arouse* desire. What is it that you *want?* They fall on deaf ears if there is nothing you want, nothing you're looking for, nothing you're hungry enough to bang on a door over. (p. 38)

Now turn the table, and imagine for a moment that you could talk to Jesus about what's on *your* heart. For that matter, think about your prayers. Do you pray? About what? What have you been asking, seeking, knocking for?

Jesus, forgive me. Why am I so guarded in my prayers? I know what I want . . . but I don't bring that to you very much at all, and certainly not with the passion and intensity that I feel it. I've really seen you as a hard person, more concerned about our morality than our hearts. Wow. To see you appeal to the desires of the people in your stories raises a hope in me that you want to speak to me about mine. Help me out of resignation. Oh, God—give me ears to hear you speaking to me about my desire.

Later in the gospel of John, Jesus extends the offer to anyone who realizes that his life just isn't touching his deep desire: "If you are thirsty, come to me! If you believe in me, come and drink! For the Scriptures declare that rivers of living water will flow out from within" (John 7:37–38 NLT). (p. 37)

How have you understood Jesus' offer here—I mean, what goes through your mind when you read this? In your own words, without trying to get the "right" answer, what does your heart think Jesus is talking about? Is it some sort of religious experience, or a manifestation of "spiritual gifts," or something about the life we'll have in heaven?

LIFE IN ALL ITS FULLNESS

Eternal life—we tend to think of it in terms of existence that never comes to an end. And the existence it seems to imply—a sort of religious experience in the sky—leaves us wondering if we *would* want it to go on forever. But Jesus is quite clear that when he speaks of eternal life, what he means is life that is absolutely wonderful and can never be diminished or stolen from you. He says, "I have come that they may have life, and have it to the full" (John 10:10 NIV). Not, "I have come to threaten you into line," or "I have come to exhaust you with a long list of demands." Not even, "I have come primarily to forgive you." But simply, *My purpose is to bring you life in all its fullness.* (p. 38)

OK—what have you done with *this* passage, with John 10:10? How do you hear it? What does Jesus mean when he says, "I have come that they may have life, and have it to the full"? And after you answer that . . . what does your answer say about your view of what God wants for you, his heart toward you?

Really? Life is really the offer? You're kidding. Why do I still doubt this so deeply? Tears well up. You really want life for me? I think I have been mistrusting your heart toward me for years. O Jesus . . . where does this mistrust come from? Why is my heart so fearful, so doubtful?

Good News That's Not Really

Things appear to have come full circle. The promise of life and the invitation to desire have again been lost beneath a pile of religious teachings that put the focus on knowledge and performance . . . Regardless of where you go to church, there is nearly always an unspoken list of what you shouldn't do (tailored to your denomination and culture, but typically rather long) and a list of what you may do (usually much shorter—mostly religious activity that seems totally unrelated to our deepest desires and leaves us only exhausted).

And this, we are told, is the good news. Know the right thing; do the right thing. This is life? When it doesn't strike us as something to get excited about, we feel we must not be spiritual enough. Perhaps once we have kept the list long enough, we will understand. (pp. 40–41)

The promise of life and the invitation to desire have again been lost beneath a pile of religious teachings. Does that sound like life to you?

"I began to seriously question my faith," wrote a friend, "when I was suffering my second year of depression. People in church saw my depressed face, and they complimented me on how I was such a good Christian." I am not making this up. This poor fellow was actually cheered for doing well spiritually when it became apparent his soul was dying. "I thought the best way for a person to live is to keep his desires to a minimum so that he will be prepared to serve God." (p. 42)

Does that sound familiar: keep your desires to a minimum, so you can serve God? How does it strike you to realize you've been handed a gospel that's, well, not really the gospel?

> Come, all you who are thirsty,
> come to the waters;
> and you who have no money,
> come, buy and eat!
> Come, buy wine and milk
> without money and without cost.
> Why spend money on what is not bread,
> and your labor on what does not satisfy?
> Listen, listen to me, and eat what is good,
> and your soul will delight in the richest of fare. (Isa. 55:1–2 NIV)

What do you think this passage is about? What in us is God appealing to?

Christianity has nothing to say to the person who is completely happy with the way things are. Its message is for those who hunger and thirst—for those who desire life as it was meant to be. (p. 43)

Read the previous passage at the bottom of page 48 over slowly, three times. Now react to it.

Good news, a report that brings us relief and joy at the same time, is news that speaks to our dilemma. Hearing from your doctor that the lump is benign is good news. Receiving a notice from the IRS that you will not be audited after all is good news. Getting a call from the police to say that they've found your daughter is good news. Being offered tips and techniques for living a more dutiful life isn't even in the field of good news. (p. 43)

Let yourself linger on this question: What news *would* bring you *relief* and *joy* right now? (Don't make it sound "spiritual"—think about your actual life.)

THE STORY OF DESIRE

I wrote about the film *Titanic* and why it was such an unprecedented, unparalleled success:

> Obviously, the film touched a nerve; it tapped into the reservoir of human longing for life . . . [It] begins with romance, a story of passionate love, set within an exciting journey. Those who saw *Titanic* will recall the scene early in the film where the two lovers are standing on the prow of the great ship as it slices through a golden sea into a luscious sunset. Romance, beauty, adventure. Eden. The life we've all been searching for because it's the life we all were made for. Have we forgotten—or never been told? Once upon a time, in the beginning of humanity's sojourn on earth, we lived in a garden that was exotic and lush, inviting and full of adventure. It was "the environment for which we were made," as the sea lion was made for the sea. Now, those of you who learned about Eden in Sunday school maybe missed something here. Using flannel graphs to depict Paradise somehow doesn't do it. Picture Maui at sunset with your dearest love. A world of intimacy and beauty and adventure. (pp. 44–45)

In all your living over the past year, has it ever *really* crossed your mind that you were meant to live in Paradise—that this life you have is not the "habitat" your heart was designed for—not even close?

Now think about the things that have "turned your head" recently, those things that have roused some hunger within you—even if they merely seemed like "temptation." Can you see in those things your longing for Eden?

Not until I put it in this context . . . but it begins to come into clarity for me. All those longings I have for freedom and romance. To travel away to some beautiful place with the Beauty of my life, to linger there for months. Do I need another vacation—maybe to a "better place" this year, somewhere exotic? I may need to get away, but when I think about those longings for escape, I see in them the echoes of what I was meant for. I'm not a freak, I'm not irresponsible . . . I'm just longing for home.

But then tragedy strikes . . . How awful, how haunting are those scenes of the slow but irreversible plunge of the great ocean liner, leaving behind a sea of humanity to freeze to death in the Arctic waters. Everything is gone—the beauty, the romance, the adventure. Paradise is lost. And we know it. More than ever before, we know it . . . The ship has gone down. We are all adrift in the water, hoping to find some wreckage to crawl upon to save ourselves. (p. 45)

And all the hassles and disappointments and deep heartaches of your life—how do you think about those? As bad luck? Probably what you deserved? Something you could have avoided if you'd just done it right? Or do you really see them as the result of living so far from Eden?

I know the Bible teaches Paradise lost—but in my daily living I think I assume I've blown it somehow, somewhere. It's never an obvious conviction, but more like an underlying feeling or "sentence," that if I were a better man, a better Christian, then life wouldn't be so hard. What a relief it would be to lift some of that false guilt. Life is shipwrecked—that's what's happened.

But that is not all. The secret of the film's success is found in the final scene. As the camera takes us once more to the bottom of the sea and we are given a last look at the rotting hulk of the once great ship, something happens. The *Titanic* begins to transform before our eyes. Light floods in through the windows. The rust and decay melt away as the pristine beauty of the ship is restored. The doors fly open, and there are all the great hearts of the story, not dead at all, but quite alive and rejoicing. A party is under way; a wedding party. The heroine, dressed in a beautiful white gown, ascends the staircase into the embrace of her lover. Everything is restored. Tragedy does not have the final word. Somehow, beyond all hope, Paradise has been regained.

Isn't this our dilemma? Isn't this the news we have been longing for? A return of the life we prize? (p. 45)

Up till this point, how *would* you have described the human dilemma, the predicament we all find ourselves in? Was it, "We're all sinners bound for hell, unless we receive God's forgiveness"? That's true, of course, but does your faith include a rich understanding of Eden, and Paradise lost? Can you see how everyone's just trying to get back some part of paradise?

And though the *objects* we choose might not be good at all—can you see that the *desire* itself is? Her life choices have been a tragic mistake, but the woman at the well's desire for love wasn't evil, was it? And now can you understand why Jesus went after her desire as the more crucial issue?

Desire and Goodness

OK—some of you are totally with me by now. You've chucked the Gospel of Sin Management for the Gospel of Life. But there are others of you who—though really drawn to the idea that desire is actually good and God-given—are still wondering about holiness and sanctification. After all, doesn't the Bible say, "Without holiness no one will see the Lord"? Indeed, it does (Heb. 12:14 NIV). Let's go on:

> Christianity takes desire seriously, far more seriously than the Stoic or the mere hedonist. Christianity refuses to budge from the fact that man was made for pleasure, that his beginning and his end is a paradise, and that the goal of living is to find Life. Jesus knows the dilemma of desire, and he speaks to it in nearly everything he says. When it comes to the moral question, it is not simply whether we say yes or no to desire, but always what we *do* with desire. (p. 46)

Warning!

So, just to make things clear, I am *not* saying that every desire that occurs to us is good, nor that we should throw caution to the wind and chase them all. As one of my favorite poets, George Herbert, says,

> [Go] not abroad at every quest and call
> Of an untrained hope or passion.
> ("Content")

As I wrote, I'm fully aware that all of us now, so far from Eden, "have desire gone mad within us." Our desire for ecstasy isn't hardwired to God, and we all know it can run in some pretty wild directions. Are you aware of a desire within you that unsettles you? What are the desires that have historically gotten you into trouble?

The lure of the beautiful woman. Like most men, there's something in me that is haunted by a memory of Eve, and when I see what I think is her, it can evoke a sense of "there—there is where life is found." It's not lust I'm describing, it's deeper than that. It's about some Eden-like allure. But from adolescence this has been one of the great false transcendences, and it has produced a great deal of false guilt. Am I not a good man?

How have you dealt with that dilemma in the past? What has been your recipe for handling desire in a godly way or, at least, to keep from getting you in trouble?

Over the years I would just knuckle down and look away. I want to be a good man, and I love my wife dearly. So I would just tough it out through raw willpower. But over the past couple of years I've found a new freedom by exploring "the desire beneath the desire," the realization that I'm not looking for another woman and I'm not desiring an affair at all. Rather, there is a deep place of transcendence in my soul that once belonged to God and Eden, and somehow I was fooled into thinking that what I sought was the beautiful woman, when in fact what I'm wanting is God. Amazing.

Tracks of a Fellow Traveler

Ecstasy and delight are essential to the believer's soul, and they promote sanctification. We were not meant to live without spiritual exhilaration, and the Christian who goes for a long time without the experience of heartwarming will soon find himself tempted to have his emotions satisfied from earthly things and not, as he ought, from the Spirit of God.

The soul is so constituted that it craves fulfillment from things outside itself and will embrace earthly joys for satisfaction when it cannot reach spiritual ones . . . The believer is in spiritual danger if he allows himself to go for any length of time without tasting the love of Christ and savoring the felt comforts of a Savior's presence. (Maurice Roberts)

God is realistic. He knows that ecstasy is *not* optional; we are made for bliss and we must have it, one way or another. He also knows that happiness is fragile and rests upon a foundation greater than happiness. All the Christian disciplines were formulated at one time or another in an attempt to heal desire's waywardness and so, by means of obedience, bring us home to bliss. (p. 47)

This journey *is* about the deepest issues of our character. How we handle desire is a deeply moral issue. But the church has really missed the boat on this one. By focusing almost totally on the *appearance* of godliness, we miss the deeper *internal* issues, the real issues of the heart. As Jesus said to the morality-equals-good-behavior crowd of his day,

Woe to you, teachers of the law and Pharisees, you hypocrites! You clean the outside of the cup and dish, but inside they are full of greed and self-indulgence. Blind Pharisee! First clean the inside of the cup and dish, and then the outside also will be clean.

Woe to you, teachers of the law and Pharisees, you hypocrites! You are like whitewashed tombs, which look beautiful on the outside but on the inside are full of dead men's bones and everything unclean. (Matt. 23:25–27 NIV)

How does Jesus feel about the Gospel of Sin Management, the approach to Christianity that focuses on *appearing* godly from the outside?

Let's get at this whole issue from another direction, using the parable of the prodigal son. Understanding that the father represents God the Father, and that the two sons are models of how people handle their desires, which son are you more like? And which son are the people in your church more like?

> Sometimes I know I'm the prodigal. At other times, I feel the arrogance of the older brother toward people who "just can't get their acts together." But as far as risking desire, most of the Christians I know are the older brother for sure. They've killed their hearts through duty, and now they're trying to take everyone else down with them.

The older brother is the picture of the man who has lived his entire life from duty and obligation. When the wayward son returns from his shipwreck of desire, his brother is furious because he gets a party and not a trip behind the barn with the broadside of a paddle. He tells his father that he has been had; that all these years he hasn't gotten a thing in return for his life of service. The father's reply cuts to the chase: "All that is mine has always been yours." In other words, "You never asked." Rembrandt captures all this powerfully in his now-famous painting *The Return of the Prodigal Son*. In the painting, the elder brother stands a step *above* the reunion of father and son. He will not step down, enter in. He is above it all. But who receives redemption? The scandalous message of the story is this: those who kill desire—the legalists, the dutiful—are not the ones who experience the father's embrace. (p. 48)

Why is that such a scandalous message—and why were the Pharisees so upset with Jesus?

The question is not, Dare we desire, but, Dare we *not* desire? (p. 48)

What might your life look like, twenty years from now, if you abandon your heart's desire and take the more conventional road of duty, obligation, and rule keeping? What will it do to your faith?

Again, finish this leg by writing out your prayer to God for the journey.

DISOWNED DESIRE

> The danger is that the soul should persuade itself that it is not
> hungry. It can only persuade itself of this by lying.
> —SIMONE WEIL

— Counsel for the Journey

We've all abandoned desires that are deep and crucial to us—even desires we know came from God. And though we are on the road to recovering and living from desire, the temptation is very real to keep it at a comfortable distance or let it slip away unnoticed. When we do, we end up living out a script someone else wrote for us. Our life is not truly our own, but a collection of expectations and demands from others.

In this leg of the journey, the goal is to discover how much of your current life is truly a reflection of your desires, so that you might begin to live with real faith and genuine hope.

— Inspiration

Another one of my (John—this will be me writing here) all-time favorite films is *Babette's Feast*. The story centers around a very devout and puritanical Christian sect whose lives and dreams have been deadened by a very mistaken view of holiness. Babette is a gourmet chef who flees Paris during the revolution and finds refuge in this little community of disowned desire. Her love and freedom, and the power of a feast she prepares, work a stunning release of their lost hearts. A beautiful film.

The sea lion loved his rock, and he even loved waiting night after night for the sea breezes that might come. Especially he loved the dreams those memories would stir. But as you well know, even the best of dreams cannot go on, and in the morning when the sea lion woke, he was still in the barren lands. Sometimes he would close his eyes and try to fall back asleep. It never seemed to work, for the sun was always very bright.

Eventually, it became too much for him to bear. He began to visit his rock only on occasion. "I have too much to do," he told himself. "I cannot waste my time just idling about." He really did not have so much to do. The truth of it was, waking so far from home was such a disappointment, he did not want to have those wonderful dreams anymore. So the day finally came when he stopped going to his rock altogether, and he no longer lifted his nose to the wind when the sea breezes blew.

A friend of mine told me last night that he used to keep a photo on his desk of him skiing off a cliff (he used to be quite a skier). But he said he can't bear to look at it anymore because it reminds him of a far more passionate time in his life, a time when his heart was much more alive . . . a time he had left behind him. So he moved the photo and turned it to the wall. Are there things in your life like that—photos, music, or places even that once stirred your heart's longings, but you no longer "visit" them? What are they—and why don't you go there anymore?

I (John) know exactly what this is for me right now—the ranch, and all that means. Just last week my father sent me some photos of my grandfather's ranch, where I lived out the golden days of my boyhood. I was ambivalent about receiving them. They feel like . . . a disruption. I don't want to go there right now—I'm too "busy." God is after me, haunting me, rousing something in my heart that I've buried. I'm not sure why I still do this, but I know that it's easier to just live life a step or two removed from my deepest desires.

The sea lion eventually found it hard to wake in the morning—he just didn't want to face the reality of the new day. Do you ever have trouble getting out of bed? What's the reason you've told yourself? Is that the *real* reason? Pay attention for a couple of days to what you feel and think when you first wake up, lying there in bed.

So the sea lion filled his life with busyness, chores, activities. Our lives, too, are full, so very busy. Is yours? How much real free time do you have in a normal week?

We say we don't like it—but I don't think that's true. If we *really* didn't like it, we wouldn't do it. Have you ever stopped to ask yourself what the *function* of all your busyness is? What does it relieve you from having to face?

O man . . . I am really nailed on this one. I know exactly what the busyness is about, because during Christmas vacation this year I wasn't busy, and all that time and space raised a bunch of issues in my soul—including how easy it is to avoid God. Not openly, not "deliberately," but it's easier to think that I'm living with real purpose and meaning when all I am is busy. I thought about Oswald Chambers, how he said that service to God is the greatest enemy of intimacy with him.

THE DOUBLE-EDGED SWORD

The chapter begins with a view of desire from the devil's point of view. On the one hand, Old Screwtape was lamenting that there were so few great sinners around anymore. It made his work much less interesting, his meals less satisfying. But, on the other hand, Screwtape decided that it's just as well to keep things that way.

> Screwtape decides that perhaps this is all for the best because there are real dangers when a soul is capable of deep desire. He knows what we have forgotten: "The great (and toothsome) sinners are made out of the very same material as those horrible phenomena, the great Saints." (p. 53)

I imagine you've got a pretty good idea what the *sinful* dangers would be if you were to recover your deep desires, venture out upon them. But have you thought about the other danger—the one the *devil* fears? What are the *good* dangers of recovering desire? What wonderful things might you do? What might be the effect on other people?

I went on to mention the lives of King David, the apostles Peter and Paul:

> The great saints come from the same material as the "toothsome sinners." Desire, a burning passion for more, is at the heart of both. (p. 53)

Why is that true—why is passion essential to both? Can you point to the lives of some of your heroes, perhaps real people, perhaps from the movies you love? Why are their lives so attractive, and so powerful? Can you name their burning desire? (And do you share it?)

BLESSED ARE THE NICE?

And so Screwtape reveals the enemy's ploy—first make humans flabby, with small passions and desires, then offer a sop to those diminished passions so that their experience is one of contentment. They know nothing of great joy or great sorrow. They are merely *nice*. One young woman wrote to me, "My parents always told me to be a 'nice little girl.' I simply assumed that being nice meant not getting upset or being angry with anyone . . . I was nice because I wanted to be liked, and I figured that people would like someone who was always nice. My senior year of high school I was voted "Nicest Senior" for the senior awards, and it was true. I was nice and I was proud of it. I thought there was no higher virtue than niceness." (p. 53)

I imagine there are many of you who can relate to this young woman. "Nice" has become one of the leading virtues in the church today. What has been the guiding principle or virtue of your Christian life? Maybe another way of asking this is, what have you wanted people to recognize you for?

The greatest enemy of holiness is not passion; it is apathy. Look at Jesus. He was no milksop. His life was charged with passion. After he drove the crooks from the temple, "his disciples remembered that it is written: 'Zeal for your house will consume me'" (John 2:17 NIV). This isn't quite the pictures we have in Sunday school, Jesus with a lamb and a child or two, looking for all the world like Mr. Rogers with a beard. The world's nicest guy. (p. 54)

Think about the image of Jesus you've had over the years. Have you imagined him as one of the most passionate persons who ever lived? That whole incident of clearing the temple of the money changers with a whip he had made himself—have you seen that as central to Jesus' personality, or more like an exception to an otherwise very nice guy?

WHAT IS IT YOU WANT?

After months of getting nowhere, I asked the obvious: "Gary, why are you a Christian?"

He sat in silence for what must have been five minutes. "I don't know. I guess because it's the right thing to do."

"Is there anything you're hoping to enjoy as a result of your faith?"

"No . . . not really."

"So what is it that you *want*, Gary?"

An even longer silence. I waited patiently. "I don't desire anything." Our sessions ended shortly thereafter, and I felt bad that I was unable to help him. You cannot help someone who doesn't want a thing. (p. 56)

Let me ask *you* that question: If you are a Christian, *why* are you a Christian? (And if you aren't, *why* aren't you?) Peter said the reason he followed Christ was because Jesus alone had "the words of eternal life" (John 6:68). Is there anything you're hoping to enjoy, a life you are hoping to find as a result of your faith?

And does your answer reflect more of a hope in a future life, as opposed to what God might do for you here and now?

Think about your prayer life for a moment. Do you pray? What about? I find in my own life that most of my prayers are prayers about needs, not about desires. My prayers for others and for myself seem to be almost exclusively about things like safety, or healing, or deliverance from evil. It's rare that I spend much time at all praying about my desires. Jot down the subject of what you've prayed for over the past several weeks or months. Was it mostly a "need" or a "desire"?

Has that begun to change as a result of this journey?

PRAYER AS THE LANGUAGE OF DESIRE

The book of Hebrews describes the prayer life of Jesus in the following way: "While Jesus was here on earth, he offered prayers and pleadings, with a loud cry and tears, to the one who could deliver him" (5:7 NLT). That doesn't sound like the way prayers are offered up in most churches on a typical Sunday morning. "Dear Lord, we thank you for this day, and we ask you to be with us in all we say and do. Amen." No pleading here, no loud cries and tears. Our prayers are cordial, modest, even reverent. Eugene Peterson calls them "cut-flower prayers." They are not like Jesus' prayers or, for that matter, like the psalms. The ranting and raving, the passion and ecstasy, the fury and desolation found in the psalms are so far from our religious expression that it seems hard to believe they were given to us as our *guide* to prayer. They seem so, well, *desperate*. (pp. 59–60)

Honestly now—how *desperate* are your prayers to God—and how *persistent?*

Lord . . . I am exposed. I feel like that king Jehoash, the guy Elijah told to hit the ground with the arrows—I give it a couple of whacks. Why do I hold back in prayer? Why? I can recall only a time or two of loud cries and tears . . . but my life is desperate. I am desperate. Oh, God, I am sick of this cautious, careful life I lead with you. I AM SICK OF IT. Help me to be more honest with you.

[I want to pray more] like my son Luke. He is our youngest son and very wise for all of his five years. He knows what he wants and what it means to lose it. "My life is over." Luke laid his head down on the table and sighed, a picture of lament. I had just told him he couldn't have chocolate-covered sugar bombs for breakfast, and he was devastated. There was no longer any reason to go on. Life as he knew it was over. I enjoy Luke because he has more undisguised and unadulterated desire than anyone I know. He is "out there" with his desire and his disappointments. When we go over to someone's house for dinner, the first thing he'll ask will always be, "Is there dessert?" Part of me has tried to train this out of him; part of me admires the fact that he isn't embarrassed by his desire, like the rest of us. He is unashamed. We hide our true desire and call it maturity. Jesus is not impressed. He points to the less sophisticated attitude of a child as a better way to live. (p. 61)

How often do you confide in a friend your real desires for your life?

Would you feel comfortable if others were to read your journal here? Would you read your desires out loud to your church? Most of us wouldn't—why are we so embarrassed by our desires?

> How little we come to God with what really matters to us. How rare it is that we even admit it to ourselves. "Is there dessert?" We don't pray like Jesus because we don't allow ourselves to be nearly so *alive*. We don't allow ourselves to feel how desperate our situation truly is. We sense that our desire will undo us if we let it rise up in all its fullness. Wouldn't it be better to bury the disappointment and the yearning and just get on with life? As Larry Crabb has pointed out, pretending seems a much more reliable road to Christian maturity. (p. 61)

Has it occurred to you that most of the people you know are *pretending?!* And if that sounds a bit too dramatic, are *their* prayers filled with loud cries and tears? Are they open and vulnerable and hopeful, like Luke? Do they even talk about their deepest desires and all the struggle they bring? Name three people you know who *aren't* using denial or some level of pretending to just get on with their Christian lives.

If you know three or more of these individuals, my advice is to form a small group or home fellowship with them immediately.

DRIFTING WITHOUT DESIRE

The truth is, I had come to a point where I didn't really know what I wanted in life. My real passion had been the theater, and for a number of years I pursued that dream with great joy. I had my own theater company and loved it. Through a series of events and what felt like betrayals, I had gotten deeply hurt. I left the theater and just went off to find a job. The Washington offer came up, and even though my heart wasn't in it, I let the opinions of people I admired dictate my course. Without a deep and burning desire of our own, we will be ruled by the desires of others. (p. 62)

Let me repeat that last sentence: Without a deep and burning desire of our own, we will be ruled by the desires of others. How long has that been true for you? Think about the major you chose in college—was that your heart's desire, or was it a reflection of your parents' desires for you, or pressures of some other kind?

And how about your current occupation (including you homemakers)—is this what makes you come alive? Who chose this for you?

I believe that each one of us has a unique calling from God, a place we are made for in his great story. Furthermore, I believe our calling is reflected in our deepest desires. We'll explore this more later in the journal, but for now, do you feel you're living from your heart in your true calling? Are you closer or farther away than you were, say, five or ten years ago?

And church—how did you wind up at your current church? Is it what you really want in your relationship with God? What keeps you there? What keeps you going to church at all?

What about the clothes you wear—do they really reflect your unique tastes, or are they more what others expect you to wear?

Now let me take this to a really vulnerable place: your relationships. Think about the people you spend your free time with—do you spend time with them because you really want to, or is it more out of a sense of obligation? How many of your relationships would change if you lived from your desire?

Warning!

Many marriages come to a place where it feels like all duty and no delight. That is a tragic place to wind up, but it is *not* an excuse to break your most solemn vow ever. Even the worst marriage can be restored to life . . . through the journey of desire.

So, overall, thinking about how the hours of your days are spent—is your life right now a reflection of *your* desires, or everyone else's? It might help to give a percentage to each; say, for example, that 10 percent reflects your desires and 90 percent reflects other pressures and demands.

And if your life never changes from this point on, if this is what you have to live for the rest of your life—how would you feel about that?

Which brings us to the issue of hope.

HOPELESS WITHOUT DESIRE

To be blunt, nothing about our lives is worth asking about. There's nothing intriguing about our hopes, nothing to make anyone curious. Not that we don't have hopes; we do. We hope we'll have enough after taxes this year to take a summer vacation. We hope our kids don't wreck the car. We hope our favorite team goes to the World Series. We hope our health doesn't give out, and so on. Nothing wrong with any of those hopes; nothing unusual, either. Everyone has hopes like that, so why bother asking us? It's life as usual. Sanctified resignation has become the new abiding place of contemporary Christians. No wonder nobody asks. Do *you* want the life of any Christian you know? (p. 64)

Do you? Have a look around—whose life looks really good to you these days? Why? (Don't make this sound "spiritual." Don't say, "I want Mary's life because she is a missionary serving God," when in fact what you *really* want right now is your neighbor Julie's life because her husband loves her and she has such a beautiful home.)

> I can barely stand to be around Christians. I know that sounds harsh, but it's true. All the pretending and posing and spiritual clichés. And OK—this is going to sound a little weird. But after watching the movie Finding Forrester, about the recluse author who lives a totally private life, I've found myself thinking, Man, that looks really good. I know that's my longing for a little solitude.
>
> But if I stay with the question a bit longer, I think I'd have to say that I'd love to have Nick's wealth and his ranch—but with my heart and vision living in it.

How hopeful would you say you are these days? What are you honestly and truly hoping for? How much anticipation are you living with—a sense that your desires are coming true? (Which is a different question, by the way, than asking, "What would you love to have happen in your life, but you aren't really *expecting* to happen?" Genuine hope has an *anticipation* to it; the other kind is just sort of a passing daydream that we dismiss with a sigh of resignation.)

Looking back at your entry above, would you say those are hopes for the fulfillment of your heart's desire . . . or are they more hopes to be released from a life that's making you miserable? There's a difference. One says, "I know who I want to be and the life I was meant to live." The other replies, "I just want out of the life I have."

Now let me suggest an exercise that will take more than a few minutes—but will be worth all the time it requires, believe me. I want you to write out a description of the life you would love to be living in five years. What do you want to be doing? With whom do you want to be doing it? What is your heart truly yearning for? If your description is true to your heart, it will probably bring tears to write it out and awaken a deep battle with hope (could it be . . . ?). Give hours to this; better, give several hours over a weekend to it. Think of the things that once made your heart come alive. Think of the films you love and the lives of the characters in those films.

> ## Warning
>
> ---
>
> You might begin to feel as if, "OK, so I identify my dreams and desires . . . none of it feels attainable" and then feel tempted to bury them again because of that "it's impossible" kind of feeling. Dear friends, you cannot assess the goodness or the validity of a desire or calling based on the statistical probability of making money at it. The adventure of faith first involves identifying our heart's desire, and then staying with it and with God as *he* reveals to you how it will unfold. Let him handle the "how." You chase the "what."

FAITH AS DESIRE

You may recall the story Jesus told of the man who entrusted three of his servants with thousands of dollars (literally, "talents"), urging them to handle his affairs well while he was away. When he returned, he listened eagerly to their reports. The first two fellows went out into the marketplace and doubled their investment. As a result, they were handsomely rewarded. The third servant was not so fortunate. His gold was taken from him, and he was thrown into "outer darkness, where there will be weeping and gnashing of teeth." My goodness. Why? All he did was bury the money under the porch until his master's return. Most of us would probably agree with the path he chose—at least the money was safe there. But listen to his reasoning. Speaking to his master, he says, "I know you are a hard man, harvesting crops you didn't plant and gathering crops you didn't cultivate. I was afraid I would lose your money, so I hid it." (See Matt. 25:14–30 NLT). He was afraid of the master, whom he saw as a hard man. He didn't trust his master's heart.

The issue isn't capital gains—it's what we think of God. When we bury our desires, we are saying the same thing: "God, I don't dare desire because I fear you; I think you are hard-hearted." (pp. 57–58)

What do you think *God* thinks about your dreams and desires? More to the point, do you believe he really wants to help you reach them?

Just yesterday evening I was taking a walk in our neighborhood, talking to the Lord about going forward and establishing the ranch I have mentioned. I had been moving toward the creation of this place of ministry in what felt like sheer obedience, dragging my heart along behind me. God had been confirming the direction with many signs and affirmations. And yet I sensed that something was wrong. I was asking him what he wanted the ranch to be. He said, *What do you want it to be? What's in your heart?* I was embarrassed by the honesty of my reply: "What do you care about my desires?" There is this hurt and angry place inside, a very old wound, that harbors some rather strong doubts about how much God really cares for me.

We all have this place. Life has not turned out the way we want, and we know God could have handled things differently. Even though we may profess at one level a genuine faith in him, at another level we are like the third servant. Our obedience is not so much out of love as it is out of carefulness. (p. 58)

Are you aware of that hurt and angry place inside? What desires over the years have been precious to you, but God seemed indifferent, maybe even hostile to?

And looking at the way you handle your heart's desires now, can you see why? Most of us are cautious, guarded, careful never to expose them—not really, not deeply. How are you handling your desires nowadays?

"When the Son of Man comes, will he find faith on the earth?" Jesus had been talking about prayer by telling the story of a persistent widow who wasn't getting the justice she deserved from a belligerent judge. The woman won her case because she refused to let up. Jesus used her as a picture of unrelenting desire; he urged us not only to ask, but also to keep on asking. And then he ended the parable by wondering out loud, "When I return, will I find anyone who really lives by faith?" (see Luke 18:1–8 NIV). We know in our hearts the connection he is making, though we haven't admitted it to ourselves. To live with desire is to choose vulnerability over self-protection; to admit our desire and seek help beyond ourselves is even more vulnerable. It is an act of trust. In other words, those who know their desire and refuse to kill it, or refuse to act as though they don't need help, they are the ones who live by faith. Those who do not ask do not trust God enough to desire. *They have no faith.* The deepest moral issue is always what we, in our heart of hearts, believe about God. And nothing reveals this belief as clearly as what we do with our desire. (p. 59)

What does the way in which you handle desire tell you about your heart's *real* beliefs about God, and his heart toward you?

Again, finish this leg by writing out your prayer to God.

MOCKING OUR DESIRE— THE IMPOSTORS

The problem with desire is, you want everything.
—PAUL SIMON

— Counsel for the Journey

John closed the last chapter in the book by reminding us that when we abandon desire, it doesn't really go away—"it goes underground, to surface somewhere else at some other time . . . The danger of disowning desire is that it sets us up for a fall. We are unable to distinguish real life from a tempting imitation. We are fooled by the impostors. Eventually, we find some means of procuring a taste of the life we were meant for."

The journey of desire involves a two-part repentance all along the way. On the one hand, we repent of refusing to trust God with our desires by allowing them to surface again, allowing ourselves to admit the depths of our desire. On the other, we repent by turning from those "other lovers" that we've used to try to fill our desires or at least numb our desires so we don't have to feel them so deeply. This leg of the journey involves some honest reflection on the impostors we've chosen . . . and why.

— Inspiration

We have a sort of love/hate for the film *The Horse Whisperer*. On the one hand, it's a truly beautiful story of one man's remarkable gift with horses, and the redemption his gift brings not only to broken horses but to broken people as well. This man's relationship with horses is a picture of what Adam must have had before the Fall. And the setting in Montana is Edenlike. On the other hand, the film's story line involves an "emotional affair" of sorts—that's our caveat. But it's a classic lesson on the danger of disowned desire. The woman in question lives a life of sheer performance and control; she's killed her heart, and it gets her into trouble.

The sea lion was not entirely alone in those parts. For it was there he met the tortoise. Now this tortoise was an ancient creature, so weathered by his life in the barren lands that at first, the sea lion mistook him for a rock. He told the tortoise of his plight, hoping that this wise one might be able to help him. "Perhaps," the tortoise mused, "this is the sea." His eyes appeared to be shut against the bright sun, but he was watching the sea lion very closely. The sea lion swept his flippers once against his side, gliding to the end of the water hole and back. "I don't know," he said. "It isn't very deep." "Isn't it?" "Somehow, I thought the sea would be broader, deeper. At least, I hoped so."

"You must learn to be happy here," the tortoise told him one day. "For it is unlikely you shall ever find this sea of yours." Deep in his old and shriveled heart, the tortoise envied the sea lion and his sea. "But I belong to the sea. We are made for each other." "Perhaps. But you have been gone so long now, the sea has probably forgotten you."

This thought had never occurred to the sea lion. But it was true, he had been gone for a long, long time. "If this is not my home, how can I ever feel at home here?" the sea lion asked. "You will, in time." The tortoise appeared to be squinting, his eyes a thin slit. "I have seen the sea, and it is no better than what you have found here." "You have seen the sea!" "Yes. Come closer," whispered the tortoise, "and I will tell you a secret. I am not a tortoise. I am a sea turtle. But I left the sea of my own accord, many years ago, in search of better things. If you stay with me, I will tell you stories of my adventures."

The stories of the ancient tortoise were enchanting and soon cast their spell upon the sea lion. As weeks passed into months, his memory of the sea faded. "The desert," whispered the tortoise, "is all that is, or was, or ever will be." When the sun grew fierce and burned his skin, the sea lion would hide in the shade of the tree, listening to the tales woven by the tortoise. When the dry winds cracked his flippers and filled his eyes with dust, the sea lion would retreat to the water hole. And so the sea lion remained, living his days between water hole and tree. The sea no longer filled his dreams.

Who is this tortoise character with counsel that seems practical, yet sets in motion the slow loss of hope?

What has he whispered to you over the years, about your desires?

That my (Craig) desires are either bad or totally unrealistic . . . therefore, don't desire; "there is no sea."

What has he whispered these past few weeks as you've been doing this journal?

It seems as though the moment I begin to articulate the desires of my heart, our ancient foe's voice is immediately saying, "All this talk of `desire' is just wishful thinking . . . `There is no sea' . . . you have nothing to offer, little to say, no one cares."

The Search Continues

I was supposed to be writing last night, but instead sat on the couch thumbing through a Williams-Sonoma catalog. It calls itself "a catalog for cooks," but really, it's a catalog of the life we wish we had. Everything is beautiful, delicious, elegant. The kitchens portrayed are immaculate—there are no messes. Cooking there would be a joy. The tables are sumptuous with their beautiful china place settings, wine glasses brimming with nectar, gourmet foods deliciously prepared, invitingly presented. Fresh flowers abound. The homes are lovely and spacious; the view out the windows is always a mountain lake, a beach, or perhaps an English garden. Everything is as it ought to be. Glancing through its pages, you get a sense of rest. Life is good. *You see,* the images whisper, *it can be done. Life is within your grasp.* (pp. 70–71)

Where does everything seem to you to be good and right? Are there catalogs, stores, Web sites, neighborhoods you find yourself lost in? Are there vacation brochures, travel shows, pretend worlds that draw you into a sense of paradise? Name them.

For so much of my life I believed life was within my grasp. I've lived with that belief and know the expectations (and demands?) it has birthed. And, of course, the anger and frustration of not achieving that which seems within reach. Driving through some neighborhoods in our area the seemingly irresistible conclusion is that if I lived in this neighborhood, with that home, that car, that amount of money (and all that comes with it . . . never having to say, "We can't afford it," traveling at will, enjoying the family cabin in the mountains . . .), life would be good, so very, very good . . . the way it's supposed to be. Though it's embarrassing to admit such blatant worldly materialism, and though I know having it all would not quench my thirst, I can get lost in the "what ifs" rather quickly. Perhaps I can't have it all, but I can have more than I do presently. Right?

And oh, how we yearn for another shot at it. Flip with me for a moment through the photo album of your heart, and collect a few of your most treasured memories. Recall a time in your life when you felt really special, a time when you *knew* you were loved. The day you got engaged perhaps. Or a childhood Christmas. Maybe a time with your grandparents. I remember one birthday in particular. My wife planned a surprise party and kept it a perfect secret. All day long, I thought everyone had forgotten me; I was thoroughly depressed. I have a hard time with birthdays anyway—the longings they rouse. I had pretty much killed my desire for something special by evening when we went to dinner at one of our favorite restaurants. There were all my friends. I was stunned, humbled, delighted all at once. It was a wonderful evening of laughter and conversation—for me, to celebrate me. A simple event, but I recall the feelings I had even still. (p. 71)

Recall a special time in your life when you were reassured of others' love for you. If you can find an actual photo, tuck it in here with your journaling.

> When our first child, our daughter Lindsey, was born, I was overwhelmed with all I think we mean when we use the word _blessed_. I was happy in a never-before-known way . . . content, excited, sobered, renewed, aware that something very dear and beyond value had been given to me. And why to me? Because someone, God, truly loved me.

Hold your memory while you gather another, a time of real adventure, such as when you first learned to ride a bike, or gallop on a horse, or perhaps did something exciting on a vacation. Stasi and I spent our tenth anniversary snorkeling in Kauai, off the Na Pali Coast. We tried to catch up to the sea turtles and grab their flippers, hoping for a ride. It was exotic and more than a little funny. I remember falling asleep that night to the sound of the waves. (pp. 71–72)

Recall a time in your life when you felt adventurous, felt excitement—and if you can find an actual photo from that time, tuck it in here with your journaling.

> I was a young boy when my family drove to a southern Utah lake for our annual family vacation. With our cabin came a boat . . . or should I say an exploration craft (in my mind a cross between a PT 109 and a hovercraft). All my young life there had always been an adult presence and supervision when we went boating;

my role was to sit still, be quiet, and stay out of the way. It was on this vacation that my dad, for the first time, let me go it alone, granting me the freedom and use of the boat. There was something heady about the validation, something risky about being free without adult supervision, and there was something wilder than imagination as I pushed off and headed to uncharted coves, weed and reed beds. Time stood still in those early nautical adventures . . .

We were meant to live in a world like that—every day. Just as our lungs are made to breathe oxygen, our souls are designed to flourish in an atmosphere rich in love and meaning, security and significance, *intimacy* and *adventure*. (p. 72)

React to John's statement above. What does this thought stir in you right now? Is it possible to flourish?

Looking for the Golden Person

Titanic roused our desire for Eden, then reaffirmed the leading alternative. It offered romantic love as the answer to the heart's deepest yearnings. The idea is that someone is out there for you, and if you can find him, his love will carry you for a lifetime . . . You don't think you've been immune to all this, do you? Culture has been chanting that mantra for a long time. Of all the films, songs, television shows, musicals, dramas, poetry, and novels you've partaken of in your life, can you name more than five in which human love is *not* held up as the pinnacle of our quest? (pp. 72–73)

Can you? List them here.

How many couples came to the altar (or dream of coming) with this expectation? "And they all lived happily ever after." We've been fed this from childhood. (p. 73)

Looking beneath the common reasons we marry, what were you looking for when *you* married? If single, what is it you hope for from marriage someday? If you do not see yourself marrying, what is it that repels you?

Lori was twenty-one; I was twenty-four when we said our vows. They were words, but they were not descriptive of our true intent. We both married to get something. I was willing to give Lori the opportunity to spend the rest of her life filling the voids in mine. Validating me as a man, making my life comfortable, supporting and cheering me on were my expectations. Twelve years later we were in counseling excavating the roots of anger, disappointment, passivity, and fear in our marriage. On our fifteenth wedding anniversary we renewed our vows, wanting to covenant again, knowing now what they truly meant.

Please understand me—of course, we long to be loved by another person. "It is not good for man to be alone." Most people live incredibly lonely lives. Our worst pain comes from our ever-present isolation. We are surrounded by people, but truly known by so few—if any. How we long for a soul-to-soul connection. But something else is going on here, something at the level of *worship*.

Not long ago I received a letter from a woman whose husband had left her. Having been married for ten years, she was understandably devastated. My heart broke as she poured out the pain of her divorce. But as I read on, I became more and more concerned. She said she was weeping constantly and shaking uncontrollably. She wanted to die and was seriously considering taking her own life. It was not initial shock; the letter was penned many months after their breakup. Grief is an expected and appropriate response to the loss of love. But she was reacting as though she had lost her *life*. Which is, of course, what happens when you make someone else your life. (p. 73)

Most people don't take their search to adultery. Instead, they find other, "safer" ways to taste idyllic intimacy. It may be as subtle as that second glance or maybe never quite giving up those letters from a high-school sweetheart. When that's not enough, pornography becomes the next level for men. Most women go to fantasy, fed by romance novels, soap operas, or films such as *Titanic*. (p. 74)

Is there or has there been a "golden man" or "golden woman" in your life? What do you hope they will be/provide for you?

Tracks of a Fellow Traveler

Whenever I hear the old Frankie Avalon song "Venus," I see the blue eyes and dark hair of my first adolescent love, Kathleen. And I can feel the familiar Haunting seize my heart with palpable waves of longing and regret. We stood under the mistletoe together and I was afraid to kiss her. Even though our family moved to another state not long after, I thought for a long time it was that lost kiss that brought about the loss of the Sacred Romance; Romance that at sixteen is so embodied in first love. I felt there was something I could have done to hold on to the Sacred Romance by holding on to Kathleen. And each of us has points of contact where the transcendence of the Romance has seared our heart in the fragrance of lovers, geographies, and times. They are captured there and return to haunt us with their loss whenever we return, or are returned, to their heart locale. (Brent Curtis, The Sacred Romance)

Have you found yourself saying at some point, "If only I had married _____, life would have been so much better"? What would that "better" be?

Compare the worship given to sex and the golden other that fills nearly every film and song in our culture with the amazing professions of love and devotion to God found in the psalms:

> O God, you are my God,
> earnestly I seek you;
> my soul thirsts for you,
> my body longs for you . . .
> On my bed I remember you;
> I think of you through the watches of the night . . .
> My soul clings to you. (63:1, 6, 8 NIV)

Whom have I in heaven but you? And earth has nothing I desire besides you. (Ps. 73:25 NIV)

Could these words have been drawn from your journal? What's your reaction to these passages?

Tracks of a Fellow Traveler

Ecstasy and delight are essential to the believer's soul, and they promote sanctification. We were not meant to live without spiritual exhilaration, and the Christian who goes for a long time without the experience of heartwarming will soon find himself tempted to have his emotions satisfied from earthly things and not, as he ought, from the Spirit of God.

The soul is so constituted that it craves fulfillment from things outside itself and will embrace earthly joys for satisfaction when it cannot reach spiritual ones . . . The believer is in spiritual danger if he allows himself to go for any length of time without tasting the love of Christ and savoring the felt comforts of a Savior's presence.

When Christ ceases to fill the heart with satisfaction, our souls will go in silent search of other lovers. (Maurice Roberts)

REACHING FOR THE GOLDEN MOMENT

We do the same thing with our hunger for adventure. I imagine there must have been great excitement at the outset for those early explorers—that is, before the mosquitoes and hostile natives became realities. Most of us are not so daring; we prefer our adventure on a more modest scale. Shopping, if you can believe it, has become for most people their experience of a sort of conquest . . . Sport-utility vehicles were the top-selling line in the past ten years, but the irony is that less than 5 percent of them are ever actually taken off road. We want the illusion of adventure without really having to risk it. There is big money in outdoor gear right now; the "look" of the expedition is in. Thirty years ago you wouldn't have found a gym in every strip mall. There, in our air-conditioned sanctuaries, we tone our bodies while watching television. We'll take our adventure *vicariously*, preferring for the most part to be voyeurs of the extreme sport rage or our favorite sports teams. (pp. 76–77)

What modest adventures do you embark upon? Clothes that give you an image of attractiveness, equipment to provide excitement? What provides the illusion of adventure without really having to risk it? What image are you purchasing and presenting?

Don't be fooled by the apparent innocence of the object you've chosen. What is its *function?* Most of our idols also have a perfectly legitimate place in our lives. That's their cover. That's how we get away with our infidelity . . . We don't want to take a good, hard look at what we are really doing, for then we might see the lie. We would expose the impostors. We would see the water hole for the muddy puddle it is. Our idols become the *means* by which we forget who we truly are and where we truly come from. They numb us . . . When the going gets tough, the tough go shopping or fishing or out to dinner. They're all impostors—every one. But we're so taken by the dizzying array of choices, we never have to stop and take a good look at what we're doing. (pp. 80, 81, 79)

Life stresses us all out, at some point or another. You have a bad day at the office. The kids are driving you crazy. Your checks bounce; your credit card is denied. When the going gets tough, where do you turn? What gives you some relief from the pressures of your life?

I've had an embarrassing idol, a bag of Cheetos, specifically, extra-crunchy Cheetos. My drive home from church passes a minimarket (my temple of doom), and many times I've stopped to temper the stress or anxiety I've felt from a day of pastoring. Tough counseling issues or difficult people raise questions about whether or not I have what it takes as a pastor. So, rather than taking the time and doing the heart work of turning to the One True God for the strength, comfort, and guidance I need, I'll reap some level of resolve and comfort by downing a quick and easy "Grab Bag" of Cheetos. And there you have it, a pastor with bright orange lips and fingers "dealing" with the painful realities of life. The momentary relief is soon overwhelmed by the shame, guilt, and embarrassment that I've settled for something so horribly short of what I truly desire.

As Dick Keyes has pointed out, most of our idols come in pairs. There is the "nearby idol," the thing close at hand, which gives us a sense of control over our world. And then there is the "faraway idol," which provides the taste of transcendence. (p. 78)

What functions as a "nearby idol" to give you a sense of control over your world? Is it money, looks, intelligence, hard work, faithful Christian "service"? And what's your "faraway idol"—which provides a taste of transcendence? Is it a dream you never chase but never let go of, either? Is it the opinions of others, or escape through some fantasy life?

THE NARCOTIC OF PLEASURE

G. K. Chesterton thought that everybody ought to get drunk once a year because if that didn't do you good, the repentance in the morning would. There's nothing like waking up to what you've done, whether it's having too much to drink or eat, or letting your anger fly. The remorse after a flagrant sin often does bring a sense of clarity and resolution. (How many New Year's resolutions are made the morning after?) But if we don't quite overdo it, if we keep our indulgence at a more moderate level, such clarity never comes. We never see it in black and white, for we're always under the influence. No one stops to think about it. Pleasure isn't nearly so much about true enjoyment as it is about anesthetizing ourselves. (p. 79)

Think about the relief your idols provide—is your desire truly and deeply satisfied, or does the relief come more through the temporary *absence* of desire?

I've had a nagging sense I was more pleasure-oriented than might be good, but I didn't see the function of pleasure in my life until I had to face intense grief and loss. I tried every drug I could, and nothing worked. Not food. Not sleep. Not work. Not reading. Not even sex. I could not get away from the pain. And then it occurred to me: If I am trying to use pleasure as a drug in this case, how many of my so-called enjoyments are merely the same thing on a lesser scale? (p. 79)

How much of your so-called free time is really just an attempt to *numb* yourself from feeling anything? Is TV really enriching your soul? Is overeating really touching your heart's deepest longing? Is straightening the garage or ironing the sheets really necessary?

The ache for more urges me on, while the uneasiness of such strong longings persists. An uneasiness that is fed by the many good Christian friends who seem very content with life as it is . . . seemingly desiring very little. I forget that desire is God's design for me. Woven into my being is this need, these yearnings and cravings . . . for something deeper, weightier, truer than anything I've embraced thus far. How long can we hold off desire when it seems to demand satisfaction? The choice seems to be to kill desire by settling for something less . . . yet, nonetheless pleasurable.

THE ASSAULT ON OUR DESIRE

"You must learn to be happy here," the tortoise told him one day. "For it is unlikely you shall ever find this sea of yours."

The constant effort to arouse our desire and capture it can be described only as an assault. From the time we get up to the time we go to bed, we are inundated with one underlying message: *it can be done.* The life you are longing for *can* be achieved. Only buy this product, see this movie, drive this car, take this vacation, join this gym, what have you. The only disagreement is over the means, but everyone agrees on the end: we can find life now. (p. 83)

Advertisers know we're looking for the Golden Person, the Golden Moment, the Golden Something that satisfies our quest . . . and they know we'll buy anything, do anything, or go anywhere if we think we might grasp it. Watch an evening of television, paying attention to the commercials. What do the advertisers know about you—and what are they trying to convince you of?

Tracks of a Fellow Traveler

Infomercials, business seminars (with testimonials), self-help and how-to books are EVERYWHERE. Everyone is asking the question, "How did so-and-so get their life together? I want the formula." Countless products and business strategies claim to pave the way to a pain-free, foolproof plan for life, love, beauty, and wealth. It is the most potent, seductive culture spreading from the U.S. and across the world. Money is spent, attempts are made to change behaviors . . . yet no one pays any attention to the heart, to desire, or to the One who created both for transformation. That whole way of life is godless. (Jen)

I suppose the architects of Madison Avenue are for the most part motivated merely by success. It's their job to sell. But behind the whole mimetic madness is an even more brilliant schemer. The evil one has basically two ploys. If he cannot get us to kill our hearts and bury our desire, then he is delighted to seduce our desire into a trap. Once we give over our desire for life to any object other than God, we become ensnared . . . It is truly diabolical. We wind up serving our desire slavishly, or resenting it, or a little of both. (pp. 83–84)

What is the evil one, the "tortoise" in your life, trying to get you to do with your desire these days? Is it working?

OUR TIMING IS OFF

The sea no longer filled his dreams.

It was three days after Brent's fall, and I was talking to a mutual friend of ours on the phone, telling him what I had been feeling—anger, rage, grief, numbness, exhaustion. Dan said, "And envy." He went on to describe his own feelings of a sort of jealousy, that Brent was home, that he had moved "from the battle to the banquet." I didn't reply. I didn't know what to say. I wasn't feeling envy; it hadn't even crossed my mind. Certainly, part of that can be written off to what I was going through. But not all of it. (p. 85)

By this point in your life you've probably been to several funerals. Have you ever felt *envy* for those who have died? Has it even crossed your mind?

Dan's comment exposed my basic commitment to find life here and now. It is a commitment nearly all of us share, at a far deeper level than we'd like to admit. There's something just a little hurt and angry in all of us as we find that life is not coming through. (p. 85)

Can you see that demand working in your life?

For longer than I want to admit, many of my battles have sprung from an impatience with God's timing for our ultimate joy. I find myself at times in a demanding posture that insists on euphoria. I put off the reality checks of living within a budget and will impulse shop for some intoxicating new toy. I can crank the tunes and lose myself in the bliss of a musical diversion. I'll run to friends as an alternative to some responsible demand. The truth that much of what I truly desire must await heaven seems to fuel the need to get a little something to "tide me over" in the here and now.

Although our desire has taken us to a thousand "other lovers," we must not make a fatal error and try one more time to get rid of it. We cannot revert to killing our hearts. Instead, we must accept the first lesson in the journey of desire: ecstasy is *not* optional. We must have life. The only problem is in our refusal to wait. That is why God must rescue us from the very things we thought would save us. (p. 86)

In some ways, all our work up to this point has been to make that one truth and deep reality written on our hearts: We Must Have Life. Our desire tells us it's true. We cannot live only from a sense of duty and obligation. We cannot live a script written for us by others. We must have life. Do you see it more clearly now?

Tracks of a Fellow Traveler

Father, I want to know Thee, but my coward heart fears to give up its toys. I cannot part with them without inward bleeding, and I do not try to hide from Thee the terror of the parting. I come trembling, but I do come. Please root from my heart all those things which I have cherished so long and which have become a very part of my living self, so that Thou mayest enter and dwell there without a rival. Then shalt Thou make the place of Thy feet glorious. Then shall my heart have no need of the sun to shine in it, for Thyself wilt be the light of it, and there shall be no night there. In Jesus' Name, Amen. (A. W. Tozer)

Write out the prayer your heart is stirred to from this section.

THE DIVINE THWARTER

Someone has altered the script.
My lines have been changed . . .
I thought I was writing this play.
—MADELEINE L'ENGLE

Devise your plan. It will be thwarted.
—GOD

━ Counsel for the Journey

The leg you are about to embark on is probably the greatest source of confusion and pain in most people's lives. Why would God make life so hard? Why won't he just grant me what I desire? Why would he actually set himself against the very things that are so precious to me? As Oswald Chambers says, it is here, in the valleys of our lives, that most of us lose heart and give up. That's why it is *so* important for you to think through these issues.

And as you do, keep this one central truth in mind: God is committed to the healing and the freedom of your heart (Isa. 61:1–3). He really is *for* you. When you uncover places of hurt or even a sense of betrayal, hold this truth up as a candle to light your way.

━ Inspiration

If you haven't read *The Sacred Romance* (or even if you have), I (John) think you'll find the chapter on The Wildness of God to be a big help in understanding how and why God thwarts us.

It was in May that the winds began to blow. The sea lion had grown used to wind, and at first he did not pay much heed at all. Years of desert life had taught him to turn his back in the direction from which the wind came and cover his eyes with his flippers, so that the dust would not get in. Eventually, the winds would always pass.

But not this time. Day and night it came, howling across the barren lands. There was nothing to stop its fury, nothing to even slow it down. For forty days and forty nights the wind blew. And then, just as suddenly as it had begun, it stopped. The sea lion lifted himself to have a look around. He could hardly believe his eyes.

Every single leaf had been stripped from his tree. The branches that remained, with only a twig or two upon them, looked like an old scarecrow. And I do not need to tell you that there was no longer any shade in which to hide. But worse than this, much worse indeed, was what the sea lion saw next. The water hole was completely dry.

Why did God do this to the sea lion? And what's your reaction to his story?

Has God ever done anything like this to you—taken something away, thwarted something? What was it? What happened—how did it make you feel? And what was your response?

What do you privately fear he *might* take away? And why did you choose that?

I (John) fear he'll take away my ministry, my writing and speaking and the wonderful effects it has on others' lives. I fear I'll "dry up" creatively, have nothing more to say. Why did I pick that? I dunno. Partly because it's one of the greatest joys in my life and I fear that I may be getting attached to it, deriving too much of my identity from it. Deeper, I think I fear that someday everything's just going to cave in—that life can't go on this well forever.

SETTING FORTH

This yearly [fly fishing] pilgrimage has always been for me a time of consummate pleasure, a banquet of beauty with deep friendship and adventure. Then it all began to unravel. I had scheduled a few days on the Frying Pan River in Colorado in late May. The fishing there is legendary, and recent reports had been phenomenal. But as a friend and I drove up to the river, it began to rain. *Not to worry*, I thought. *Late spring often brings rain. It'll blow over in an hour or two.* As we climbed into the mountains, the rain turned into a snowstorm that lasted the entire trip.

I began to play chess with God. The following year, I planned our trip for July to eliminate all possibility of snow. I booked several days at a private ranch that caters to fly fishermen, with a guide to take us out on the upper Rio Grande. The night before we were to leave, I received a call telling me that, no, it had not snowed, but thunderstorms had created mudslides and the fishing was impossible. They offered to refund my money.

I sensed that God had made a countermove, and that my king was in danger. Grabbing my phone book, I found the number of another guide on a different river and called him. Yes, the fishing was fabulous. Yes, he could take us out tomorrow. I hung up the phone with a smile. Your move, God. When we arrived early the next morning, the fellow told us sadly, "It's the strangest thing, but they opened the dam last night and the river's flooded. Sorry 'bout that."

The next year it was a drought; the year after that we still don't know what happened. High in the meadows of the Eastern Sierra, the fish had seemed to simply vanish from the San Joaquin. I was losing the game, as you can tell. But I hadn't been cornered; not yet. (pp. 89–90)

What might you be playing chess with God over? What are you scrambling to make sure you get—or if you've gotten it, that you don't lose it? Is it the same thing you mentioned above, that you inwardly fear God might take away?

Good grief—tonight it was something really silly. From time to time I enjoy a glass of wine with dinner. Tonight I sensed God was saying to abstain for a while. I was mad. I don't want to give up my little pleasures and comforts. My irritation was so telling. I know he was showing me that the same dynamic is at work in other—major—areas of my life. I don't want to let go of the things I've found that bring me pleasure, or happiness, or a sense of security or identity. Ugh. I'm grasping again.

CRUEL OR KIND?

This is the point at which God most feels like our enemy. It seems at times that he will go to any length to thwart the very thing we most deeply want. We can't get a job. Our attempt to find a spouse never pans out. The doctors aren't able to help us with our infertility. Isn't this precisely the reason we fear to desire in the first place? Life is hard enough as it is, but to think that God himself is working against us is more than disheartening. As Job cried out, "What do you gain by oppressing me? . . . You hunt me like a lion and display your awesome power against me" (10:3, 16 NLT). (p. 91)

Warning!

I want to state very clearly that not every trial in our lives is specially arranged for us by God. Much of the heartache we know simply comes from living in a broken world filled with broken people. And we have an enemy in the evil one, who hates us deeply. Jesus warns us that Satan comes against us "to steal and kill and destroy," but that God's overall purpose is to bring us life (John 10:10 NIV).

Yet there are times when God seems to be set *against* us. Unless we understand our desperate hearts and our incredible tenacity to arrange for the life we want, events like these will just seem cruel.

Which of your prayers has God just not answered? What needs or desires has he seemed to ignore? What is your heart's real reaction to that?

When we lived in Eden, there was virtually no restriction on the pleasure around us. We could eat *freely* from any tree in the Garden. Our desire was innocent and fully satisfied. I cannot even imagine what five minutes in total bliss would be like. We had it all, but we threw it away. By mistrusting God's heart, by reaching to take control of what we wanted, Adam and Eve set in motion a process in our hearts, a desperate grasping that can be described only as *addiction*. Desire goes mad within us. (p. 92)

Do you know what that means—have you experienced firsthand what it's like to have desire "go mad" within you, pull you into something you wouldn't in your right mind have chosen?

Addiction may seem too strong a term to some of you. The woman who is serving so faithfully at church—surely, there's nothing wrong with that. And who can blame the man who stays long at the office to provide for his family? Sure, you may look forward to the next meal more than most people do, and your hobbies can be a nuisance sometimes, but to call any of this an addiction seems to stretch the word a bit too far. (p. 93)

Does it—I mean, do you see yourself as an addict? Do you know what your addictions are these days? Or would you describe them in other terms—as "nuisances," or "slipups," or "struggles"?

And on a deeper level, what would feel like death for you to lose in your life right now? What would cause your heart to sink if God told you to give it up?

What brings you security in your life these days? Another way of asking that is, what would make you feel really vulnerable and shaky to lose?

And where are you deriving your sense of self-worth—that role or recognition that would leave you feeling like a failure or lost, if you lost it tomorrow?

I have one simple response: give it up. If you don't think you're a chess player, too, then prove it by letting go of the things that provide you with a sense of security, or comfort, or excitement, or relief. You will soon discover the tentacles of attachment deep in your own soul. There will be an anxiousness; you'll begin to think about work or food or golf even more. Withdrawal will set in. If you can make it a week or two out of sheer willpower, you will find a sadness growing in your soul, a deep sense of loss. Lethargy and a lack of motivation follow. (p. 93)

Do it. Give up even those "innocent" pleasures for just one week, and notice what happens. In fact, notice your reaction to my merely *suggesting* you give those pleasures up, and write it down here.

I'm irritated. Life is hard enough as it is, without my imposing "unnecessary" restrictions on my comforts too. I love Christmas; I hate Lent. That reveals a lot.

ON THE CURSE FOR MEN

God thwarts men where it hurts most—in the field. He strikes a blow in the arena of our labor, our strength. This is our most vulnerable spot. We draw our sense of worth from it. I am not minimizing the importance of intimacy to a man; not at all. But when men get together, they don't talk about how everyone's relationship is doing. "Did you hear about Sally and Bill? I wonder if everything's okay. Maybe we should give them a call." No, they talk about their *achievements* (typically with a little embellishment). "I bagged the Zonax account today. Yep. Won't be long now before I'm running Sales." A man's impostors are most often born out of this place in his heart. Either they offer a false sense of strength, or they relieve a man from having to be strong. Pornography, for example, does both. The woman says, "I will make you feel like a man by giving myself to you, and you don't have to do anything at all. You can have the pleasure of a woman without having to *live* with her." A man's deepest desires always relate to his strength, one way or another, and so the curse for a man strikes him at the core. (p. 94)

Both men and women—what's your reaction to this idea of the curse for a man?

Men—what *do* you most fear? Name one or two of the worst things that could happen in your life.

Every man knows the reality of the curse because every man must face the ongoing frustration of *futility* and *failure*. No matter how much a man achieves, it is never enough. He has to go out tomorrow and do it all again. If you hit a home run in last week's game, there is such a short time of joy. Next time you're at the plate, everyone expects you to do it again. And again. Futility. (p. 95)

Men—what area in your life really feels futile, like no matter how much you give, you'll never get on top of it?

And even if you do seem to beat the odds and secure yourself financially, the curse is waiting for you somewhere else in your life—in your marriage or with your children. That is why a man's worst fear is not measuring up. A woman isn't affected by defeat the way a man is. It may hurt, but typically, she bounces back from failure. Not so for a man; in some cases, failure can be debilitating for life. (p. 95)

Again, for the men—what have been some of the worst failures in your life? How did you handle them? Did you bounce right back, or did it take time? Or have you abandoned that arena altogether?

Have you had a recent failure or setback? What did you do afterward in order to find a little relief?

ON THE CURSE FOR WOMEN

Every woman knows the reality of the curse because every woman lives with *relational heartache* and *loneliness*. With the skill of a surgeon going after a cancer, God thwarts a woman where it matters most—in her relationships. Are not her deepest tears shed over issues of failed intimacy? When women get together, they don't talk about work, unless it's to talk about their work *relationships*. This observance is not condescending in the least. A woman's glory is her heart for others, her keen sense of interpersonal dynamics, her commitment to maintaining relational connections. A woman who knows she is deeply loved typically survives a career setback that would send a man into a tailspin. (pp. 95–96)

Both men and women—what's your reaction to this idea of the curse for a woman?

Ladies—what have been your worst heartaches over the years? Can you name them now—and do you see the relational side to them?

Have you had a recent relational failure or rejection? What did you do afterward in order to find a little relief?

What do *you* most fear as a woman? What are one or two of the worst things that could happen in your life?

A woman's impostors are nearly always an attempt to somehow fill that ache for love or pretend she doesn't need love . . . The worst fear for a woman is *abandonment.* Like a man who refuses to play the man for fear of failing, a woman who shuns intimacy only reveals her fear of rejection by refusing to face it honestly, openly. As for the love substitutes, men aren't buying Danielle Steele romances. They have to be dragged to the next "love finally finds her" movie. Women often create colorful fantasy worlds, a kind of pornography that guarantees rich intimacy in spite of the emptiness of daily life. The writers of soaps know this tendency only too well. (p. 96)

What are your fantasies as a woman? Where do you go to find a little intimacy?

And if all this talk of relationships seems untrue for you, let me ask—would you end your life in happiness if you were never, ever really *pursued* as a woman?

THE HARDEST LESSON TO LEARN

God *promises* every man futility and failure; he *guarantees* every woman relational heartache and loneliness. We spend most of our waking hours attempting to end-run the curse. We will fight this truth with all we've got. Sure, other people suffer defeat. Other people face loneliness. But not me. I can beat the odds . . . Isn't there something defensive that rises up in you at the idea that you cannot make life work out? Isn't there something just a little bit stubborn, an inner voice that says, *I can do it?* (pp. 96–97)

Is there?

You bet there is. I'm not going down, not without a fight. I don't even like all this talk about the curse. I want life, and I want it now.

It can't be done. No matter how hard we try, no matter how clever our plan, we cannot arrange for the life we desire. Set the book down for a moment and ask yourself this question: Will life ever be what I so deeply want it to be, in a way that cannot be lost? (p. 97)

Do it, right now. Read that statement over slowly several times, until it sinks into your heart . . . and let yourself have an unedited response. Then pick up the journal and record what came up.

This is the second lesson we must learn, and in many ways the hardest to accept. We must have life; we cannot arrange for it. People will avoid this lesson all their days, changing their plans, their jobs, even their mates, rather than facing the truth. "You were wearied by all your ways, but you would not say 'It is hopeless.' You found renewal of your strength, and so you did not faint" (Isa. 57:10 NIV). These are the majority of folks out there, Christian and pagan, who are still giving it a go. Yes, a smaller number have collided against failure and heartache in such a devastating way that they have come to see it can't be done, but they have faded into resignation, or bitterness, or despair. They have taken their revenge on the God who has thwarted them by killing their desire. (pp. 97–98)

So—there are three categories of people in this world (and in the church): (1) those who still believe they can arrange for life, (2) those who know they can't and so they've given up even wanting life, and (3) those who are longing for life, know they can't arrange for it, and are looking to God to bring them life. Which do you fall in? Which do your closest family and friends fall in?

"Remember how the LORD your God led you all the way in the desert these forty years, to humble you and to test you in order to know what was in your heart . . . He humbled you, causing you to hunger" (Deut. 8:2–3 NIV). When the Israelites left Egypt, they headed across the Red Sea to Mount Sinai. From there it was only about a two-week journey into the promised land. Fourteen days turned into *forty years*. A blind camel would have found its way sooner than that. God designed a supernaturally long trail in order to deal with what was in their hearts. (p. 99)

How do you like that idea—that God has also designed a trail of waiting and hardship and disappointment for you, to see what is in your heart? Do you know what that trail is?

God must take away the heaven we create, or it will become our hell. You may not think your efforts to arrange for a little of what you desire are anything like heaven on earth. I certainly didn't; not, at least, in the more conscious regions of my heart. But some deep and tender part of us gets trapped there in those times and places where we have had a taste of the life we long for. There in the ranch lands of central Oregon, I realized that the real issue is this: I haven't wanted to be an eternal person. I've wanted to find life here somehow. And not somehow, but through golden days on western streams, with men I love. For it was there I felt most alive, most loved, most hopeful. (p. 100)

And what have the disappointments and the heartaches been bringing up in your heart? Can you see what God has been after in you, in a personal way?

Many people were shattered by Brent's death. I know I was. Not even on my worst enemies would I wish such pain. But I also know this: the shattering was good. Living apart from God comes naturally; all the striving and arranging is so second nature to me that to have it stopped in its tracks was a great good. I would wake in the morning in those early days of grief, and instead of my desires "rushing at me like a pack of wild animals" as Lewis said, I knew *it can't be done*. I knew it more deeply and more personally than I had ever known it before. We must learn this lesson, at whatever cost, or the spell will not be broken and we will never discover true hope. (p. 103)

Have you come to the place where you can say, honestly and not just because it's the right thing to say, "God . . . thank you for thwarting me"?

HOPE

How do we accept that *it can't be done* with an open heart? How do we sustain desire in the face of ongoing failure and loneliness? It all depends on what we do with hope. (p. 98)

Hope is everything in sustaining the life of our deep heart. Would you describe yourself as a hopeful person? One of the most hopeful people you know?

"In this world you will have trouble. But take heart! I have overcome the world"
(John 16:33 NIV).

What's your first-pass reaction to reading that passage?

"Set your hope *fully* on the grace to be given you when Jesus Christ is revealed"
(1 Peter 1:13 NIV, emphasis added). I read a passage like this, and I don't know
whether to laugh or to cry. Fully? We don't even set our hope *partially* on the life
to come. Not really, not in the desires of our hearts. Heaven may be coming. Great.
But it's a long way off, and who really knows, so I'm getting what I can now. Our
search is limited only by our finances, our options, and our morals. Those with fewer
misgivings and greater financial discretion go farther with it. For most Christians,
heaven is a backup plan. (pp. 98–99)

Honestly, now—how often do you think about heaven?

How many books on heaven have you read in your life?

How many conversations have you initiated with close friends about heaven?

Tracks of a Fellow Traveler

Louis Berkhof in his Systematic Theology, a tome of 738 pages, devotes only one page to heaven and two pages to hell. (Millard J. Erickson)

"We are never living, but hoping to live; and whilst we are always preparing to be happy, it is certain, we never shall be so, if we aspire to no other happiness than what can be enjoyed in this life" [Pascal].

What are you looking forward to in the next few months?

What are you looking forward to over the next few years?

What are you looking forward to in your retirement?

Now . . . what are you looking forward to after your death? (Have you ever written down your thoughts on that before?)

Is there a prayer you'd like to write out at this point?

THE GREAT RESTORATION

Look, I am making all things new!
—JESUS OF NAZARETH

See! The winter is past;
the rains are over and gone.
Flowers appear on the earth;
the season of singing has come.
—SONG OF SONGS 2:11–12 NIV

— Counsel for the Journey

In his letter to the Colossians, the apostle Paul says that our faith and our love actually are rooted in something deeper—in our hope, the hope we have in the fabulous future that is about to be ours (1:5). But to be honest, I (Craig) know very, very few people who live with hope. For most people, the future is limited to the next few days or weeks or maybe years. Heaven is either a blank or a weak promise of religious abstractions.

Our hearts cannot live without hope. As John said in *The Sacred Romance*, hope is to our soul like breathing is to our body. We've got to have it; hope is not optional. Without hope I'm an insatiable hedonist trying to put off the despair circling my perimeter. With hope I am alive, more aware of a "larger story" and more passionate about it capturing my everyday focus (less consumed by my "smaller story"). I find myself more willing to acknowledge the mysteries of suffering and brokenness . . . more accepting that some problems in life are presently unfixable. Hope gives me a context that gives my life a sense of roominess.

In the next three chapters we want your heart to be stunned and surprised at how the life you've always longed for really *is* the life that God has promised to you.

— *Inspiration*

"These Are Days" is a hope-inspired, hope-filled song about the return of spring in our lives. It could have been written to go with this chapter. By 10,000 Maniacs (I know, it sounds weird, but you'll love this song and play it in your car for weeks) off the *Our Time in Eden* CD.

And may I (Craig) recommend a surprising film as well—*The Lion King?* It contains one of the most powerful pictures of a beautiful kingdom (lush Africa), a kingdom lost to evil, and, at the end, the kingdom restored as it was meant to be. Just ignore the "circle of life" stuff and notice how the film is based on the gospel message. Watch the first five minutes and the last ten— it's the Great Restoration.

SETTING FORTH

I was walking in the woods and fields behind our house one evening, four months after Brent's death. My heart was so aware of the loss—not only of Brent, but in some ways, of everything that mattered. I knew that one by one, I would lose everyone I cared about and the life I am still seeking. (p. 107)

What does the thought of being vulnerable to the loss of the people and things that are close to your heart stir in you? Where do these reflections take you? Into anxiety, some level of the blues, or depression, anger, resignation, an awareness and comforting trust in God's goodness?

At first blush I (Craig) find myself hesitant to give myself to the question. I'd prefer to quickly dismiss any serious reflection with a firm confession that life is unpredictable yet God is always present, and can be found sufficient to meet all my needs. My hiding behind truth doesn't squelch the more personal answer. It scares me. To lose those closest to me seems overwhelming . . . beyond my ability and God's ability to deal with. I so quickly waffle between the thoughts, But God would never allow anything like that to happen (we'll all live to a ripe old age, no health restrictions, dying peacefully in our sleep), and You know he's (God) going to get you, maybe not today, maybe not tomorrow, but it's inevitable . . . you'll be another Job.

At a wedding I was officiating I asked, "Who gives this woman to be married to this man?" Standing next to the bride, facing me, was her brother. With a strong voice, both proud and sad, he said, "I do. On behalf of her family, and if her father were still alive he would with his blessing." She teared up; so did I. At the happiest moment in her young life the painful reality of her father's absence laced everything (he had died in a tragic airplane crash earlier that year). I ached for her pain and feared for my daughters.

Telling myself to long for eternity feels like telling myself to let go of all I love— forever. It feels like accepting the teaching of Eastern religions, a *denial* of life and all God created. We lose it all too soon, before we can begin to live and love. (p. 108)

Does it feel that way to you sometimes too?

THE SECRET OF SPRING

Winter tarries long at six thousand feet. Here in the Rocky Mountains, spring comes late and fitfully. (p. 108)

What "winters" of life have you journeyed through already? Write out some of your recollections from those cold, dark days of pain, loss, resignation, disorientation . . . malaise of heart. If you haven't been through a "winter," what would one look like in your life?

Going back through previous journals quickly reminded me of one recent bitter winter. Our daughters' adolescence: so many, too many, early mornings I felt the jagged edge of a daughter's scornful dismissing rejection. I wrote then, "How fierce the pain my daughters cause. There seems to be no hope, and worse, no relief. They take all they can, wanting more, scorning our imperfect attempts to engage relationship. We are, to them, Law; we are boundaries; we are limited resources. We are life's cruel limits and consequences. They hate us, as I do." Later: "Right now, it seems to be a severe season with the girls. The poison and venom of a man who insists upon an orderly, pleasant world is being exposed by uncooperative kids." "If she knew how vicious her passive-aggressive adolescence was she would, I hope, fall on her knees and repent of murder." What a cold season it was: "My soul was so distressed with anger, fear, and anxiety yesterday. At one moment I felt as if I was spinning out of control, headed for destruction, certain destruction both in this life and for eternity."

And then, just this afternoon, I rounded the corner into our neighborhood, and suddenly, the world was green again. The bluffs behind our house were transformed. What had been rock and twig and dead mulch was a rich oriental carpet of green. I was shocked, stunned. How did it happen? As if in disbelief, I got out of my car and began to walk through the woods, touching every leaf. Just yesterday the scrub oaks had the twisted, gnarled look of the hands of an old witch. Now they are beautiful, tender, supple like a maiden. The birds are back as well, waking us in the morning with their glad songs. All the chirps and cheeps and whistles and twitters, a raucous melody of simple joy. It happened suddenly. In the twinkling of an eye. (p. 109)

Has spring come for you? Has winter ended? Put words to it. Perhaps you are still in a time of winter—what would you hope for spring to bring?

Spring caught me by surprise. It was long in coming but it did. Seemingly in a day, specifically her eighteenth birthday, something shifted. Was it in her? Had some invisible hormone drip run dry or been turned off? Or did some incredible transformation take root in my soul as a father that earned my deliverance? She was, once again, "back" (Thank you, merciful Christ Jesus). My lovely girl. Just this week she wrote me a wonderful love note . . . it's tucked into my journal and forever in my heart.

My surprise is telling. It seems natural to long for spring; it is another thing to be completely stunned by its return. I am truly and genuinely surprised, as if my reaction were, *Really? What are you doing here?* And then I realized, *I never thought I'd see you again.* I think in some deep place inside, I had accepted the fact that winter is what is really true. As I lived through the first year of my grief, I had unconsciously settled into resignation. Empty and still, the world outside seemed a confirmation, the only fitting backdrop to the world within. I am shocked by the return of spring. And I wonder, *Can the same thing happen for my soul?* (p. 109)

Has the "winter" of life felt more true than "spring" for you? Write out your thoughts about what seems more true for you . . . and why.

Tracks of a Fellow Traveler

I think we have lost the old knowledge that happiness is overrated—that, in a way, life is overrated. We have lost somehow a sense of mystery—about us, our purpose, our meaning, our role. Our ancestors believed in two worlds, and understood this to be the solitary, poor, nasty, brutish and short one. We are the first generation of man that actually expected to find happiness here on earth, and our search for it has caused such unhappiness. The reason: if you do not believe in another, higher world, if you believe only in the flat material world around you, if you believe that this is your only chance at happiness—if that is what you believe, then you are more than disappointed when the world does not give you a good measure of its riches, you are in despair. (Dwight Moody, Heaven)

MORE THAN CHURCH FOREVER

But of course we aspire to happiness we can enjoy now. Our hearts have no place else to go. We have made a nothing of eternity. If I told you that your income would triple next year, and that European vacation you've wanted is just around the corner, you'd be excited, hopeful. The future would look promising. It seems possible, *desirable*. But our ideas of heaven, while possible, aren't all that desirable. Whatever it is we think is coming in the next season of our existence, we don't think it is worth getting all that excited about. We make a nothing of eternity by enlarging the significance of this life and by diminishing the reality of what the next life is all about. (pp. 110–11)

At this point in your journey, does heaven excite you? Why . . . or why not?

What would lead you to a deeper excitement about heaven, a longing for eternity?

I recall as a young pastor visiting a middle-aged man dying of cancer. His death was imminent. I was startled by his deep confidence, warm acceptance, and pure excitement about dying AND going to heaven. What shocked me was my apparent unbelief in a future. Though outwardly I performed my ministerial duty of comforting the sick and dying, inwardly I couldn't help but think, He's leaving his young children, his wife . . . everything, and he's excited? I wouldn't be. Over the years the hope of heaven has begun to embrace me. I've gotten a whiff of its shores and find myself yearning to come ashore.

Nearly every Christian I have spoken with has some idea that eternity is an unending church service. After all, the Bible says that the saints "worship God in heaven," and without giving it much more thought we have settled on an image of the never-ending sing-along in the sky, one great hymn after another, forever and ever, amen.

And our heart sinks. *Forever and ever? That's it? That's the good news?* And then we sigh and feel guilty that we are not more "spiritual." We lose heart, and we turn once more to the present to find what life we can. Eternity ends up having no bearing on our search for life whatsoever. It feels like the end of the search. And since we're not all that sure about what comes after, we search hard now. Remember, *we can only hope for what we desire.* How can the church service that never ends be more desirable than the richest experiences of life here? It would be no small difference if you knew in your heart that the life you prize is just around the corner, that your deepest desires have been whispering to you all along about what's coming to you. You see, Scripture tells us that God has "set eternity" in our hearts (Eccl. 3:11 NIV). Where in our hearts? In our *desires.* (p. 111)

How has heaven been described for you that makes it . . . less than appealing?

Tracks of a Fellow Traveler

Our pictures of Heaven simply do not move us; they are not moving pictures. It is this aesthetic failure rather than intellectual or moral failures in our pictures of Heaven and of God that threatens faith most potently today. Our pictures of Heaven are dull, platitudinous and syrupy; therefore, so is our faith, our hope, and our love of Heaven . . . Dullness, no doubt is the strongest enemy of faith.
(Peter Kreeft)

The return of spring brings such relief and joy and anticipation. Life has returned, and with it sunshine, warmth, color, and the long summer days of adventure together. We break out the lawn chairs and the barbecue grill. We tend the garden and drink in all the beauty. We head off for vacations. Isn't this what we most deeply long for? To leave the winter of the world behind, what Shakespeare called "the winter of our discontent," and find ourselves suddenly in the open meadows of summer? (p. 111)

Throughout this book the role of nature, as it was designed to, is experienced as an arena in which God reveals innumerable insights into his character and life. When did you last take time to listen, look, touch, and breathe in the out-of-doors? To simply enjoy nature, whether sitting in a garden or standing on the helm of a sailboat cutting through the sea, and take in the simple subtle, weighty moments God may have for you. Describe a time or two you can recall, and the lesson grasped.

Tracks of a Fellow Traveler

As I stood before a flowering currant bush on a summer day there suddenly arose in me without warning, and as if from a depth not of years but of centuries, the memory of that earlier morning . . . It is difficult to find words for the sensation; of course, of desire; but desire for what? . . . and before I knew what I desired, the desire itself was gone, the whole glimpse withdrawn, the world turned commonplace again, or only stirred by a longing for the longing that had just ceased. It had taken only a moment of time; and in a certain sense everything else that has ever happened to me was insignificant by comparison.

(C. S. Lewis, Surprised by Joy: The Shape of My Early Life)

Now . . . what if spring and summer are nature's way of expressing what Jesus was in fact trying to tell us? After all, nature is God's word to us also (Rom. 1:20). If we paid close attention, we would discover something of great joy and wonder: the restoration of the world played out before us each spring and summer is *precisely* what God is promising us about our lives. (p. 112)

Just as surely as spring will come, no matter how bad the winter, the spring of your life will come as well. What does that do for your heart?

Tracks of a Fellow Traveler

These are days you'll remember
When May is rushing over you with desire . . .
It's true that you are touched by something that will grow and bloom in you.
See the signs and know their meaning.
("These Are Days" by Rob Buck and Natalie Merchant © 1992)

Life is restored to what it was meant to be. "In the beginning," back in Eden, all of creation was pronounced good because all of creation was exactly as God meant for it to be. For it to be good again is not for it to be destroyed, but healed, renewed, brought back to its goodness.

Those glimpses we see in the miracles of Jesus were the firstfruits. When he announces the full coming of the kingdom, Jesus says, "Look, I am making *all things* new!" (Rev. 21:5 NLT, emphasis added). He does not say, "I am making all new things." He means that the things that have been so badly broken will be restored and then some. "You mean I'll get a new pair of glasses?" my son Sam asked. "Or do you mean I'll get a new pair of eyes, so I won't need glasses?" What do you think? Jesus didn't hand out crutches to help the disabled. (pp. 113–14)

If life were restored to what it was meant to be, what would your life look like? What does your heart long for—somehow even know?

Does it change your view of heaven to think that what you've written *is* what will come?

OUR RESTORATION

We have an expression that we use to describe someone who's out of sorts, who's not acting like the person we know her to be: "She's just not herself today." It's a marvelous, gracious phrase, for in a very real way, no one is quite himself today. There is more to us than we have seen. I know my wife is a goddess. I know she is more beautiful than she imagines. I have seen it slip out, seen moments of her glory. Suddenly, her beauty shines through, as though a veil has been lifted. It happened one night last fall.

We had slipped away from life for a long weekend in Mexico, a time to heal and rest and just be together again. We chose a hotel away from the crowds and the *turistas*. So we were almost entirely alone one evening as we ate dinner on a veranda overlooking the Sea of Cortez. Night had fallen, and the sky was so deeply black, the stars were shining right down to the horizon of the water. We sat gazing out to sea, listening to the mariachis and the breakers and our own hearts. I turned to steal a glimpse at my wife. She was beautiful, there in the moonlight, tanned from the sun, rested, serene. She was simply beautiful in a way that life often prevents her from being, but in a way she was destined to be. (p. 116)

Tracks of a Fellow Traveler

Maybe above all [fairy tales] are tales of transformation where all creatures are revealed in the end as what they truly are—the ugly duckling becomes a great white swan, the frog is revealed to be a prince, and the beautiful but wicked

queen is unmasked in all her ugliness. They are tales of transformation where the ones who live happily ever after, as by no means everybody does in fairy tales, are transformed into what they have it in them at their best to be.
(Frederick Buechner)

In what ways is the true you different from how you live or how others may perceive you? What do you long to be truly true of you?

For a very long time I lived with a well-deserved label . . . "Craig's a comedian." I cannot count the times I've heard, "You missed your calling; you should've been a stand-up comedian." What at one time, for many reasons, I took as a compliment, now causes me to cringe. "Oh Lord," I cry, "you've made me for something grander than being the life of the party, the jokester." As that label fades, a truer, more authentic Craig is unfolding. I believe I am more of a warrior-poet than a "wise"-guy/"nice" guy . . . someone pastoral, strong, dangerous, truly compassionate.

I've spoken with many people who believe that we become "spirits" when we die; that we lose our bodies and float around. Some even believe we become angels. But I don't want to lose my body: I very much want it to be renewed. When we conceive of our future existence as something ghostly, mysterious, completely "other" than anything we've ever known, we place it beyond all hoping for. (You can only hope for what you desire.) (p. 117)

What would you love for your new body to be?

I, too, want a body . . . I'm believing that my renewed body will either be a little different or that there'll be something glorious about a few extra pounds, a receding hairline, slumped shoulders, dry skin, poor eyes, and not having a gall bladder.

Now think about this for a minute. You're the Son of God. You've just accomplished the greatest work of your life, the stunning rescue of mankind. You rose from the dead. What would you do next? Have a cookout with a few friends? It seems so unspiritual, so *ordinary*. Do you see that eternal life does not become something totally "other," but rather that life goes on—only as it should be?

Jesus did not vanish into a mystical spirituality, becoming one with the cosmic vibration. Jesus has a body, and it's *his* body. His wounds have been healed, but the scars remain—not gruesome, but lovely, a remembrance of all he did for us. His friends recognize him. They share a bite to eat. This is our future as well—our lives will be healed and we shall go on, never to taste death again. (p. 118)

What does this stir in your heart? What would you love to do after *your* resurrection?

THE EARTH IS RESTORED

The created world itself can hardly wait for what's coming next. Everything in creation is being more or less held back. God reins it in until both creation and all the creatures are ready and can be released at the same moment into the glorious times ahead. Meanwhile, the joyful anticipation deepens. (Rom. 8:19–21, *The Message*)

How wondrous this will be! Creation can be so breathtaking *now*. What shall it be like when it is released to its full glory? (p. 119)

Has something in nature taken your breath away? What was it? Journal about that experience.

We seem to have forgotten—or perhaps we've never been told—that we get the earth back as well. Too many of us have placed eternity somewhere "out there," in a wispy and ethereal "heaven" that we cannot imagine; in the clouds perhaps . . . "Behold," says the Lord, "I will create new heavens and a new earth" (Isa. 65:17; Rev. 21:1 NIV). When he says he is making all things new, he includes the earth . . . So Dallas Willard assures us, *"The life we now have as the persons we now are will continue in the universe in which we now exist."* The earth has been our home and will be our home in eternity. (pp. 120, 121–22)

Where in all the new earth would you love to visit and explore? Where would you love to live?

What do you desire in life that you fear may not be in heaven? And why wouldn't it be?

ALL SHALL BE WELL

Our search for the Golden Moment is not a search in vain; not at all. We've only had the timing wrong. We do not know exactly how God will do it, but we do know this: the kingdom of God brings restoration. The only things destroyed are the things outside God's realm—sin, disease, death. But we who are God's children, the heavens and the earth he has made, will go on. "The wolf will live with the lamb, the leopard will lie down with the goat, the calf and the lion and the yearling together" (Isa. 11:6 NIV). "And Jerusalem will be known as the Desirable Place," the place of the fulfillment of all our desires (Isa. 62:12 NLT). This is significant because it touches upon the question, What will we *do* in eternity? If all we've got are halos and harps, our options are pretty limited. But to have the whole cosmos before us—wow. Thus George MacDonald writes to his daughter, whom he will soon lose to tuberculosis,

> I do live expecting great things in the life that is ripening for me and all mine—when we shall have all the universe for our own, and be good merry helpful children in the great house of our father. Then, darling, you

and I and all will have the grand liberty wherewith Christ makes free—
opening his hand to send us out like white doves to range the universe.
(*The Heart of George MacDonald*) (p. 123)

It's time to start making some plans for that day. What would you love to do in the
fully restored kingdom of God, as a fully restored man or woman?

Having finished this chapter, what's in your heart right now to do? Is it to journal,
pray, go for a run, have coffee with a friend, write a song, paint a picture, go for a walk,
read a book? Do it!

Tracks of a Fellow Traveler

Somewhere over the rainbow
Skies are blue,
And the dreams that you dare to dream
Really do come true.
(Dorothy, The Wizard of Oz)

THE GRAND AFFAIR

And the people came together, and the people came to dance,
and they danced like a wave upon the sea.
—WILLIAM BUTLER YEATS

‒ *Counsel for the Journey*

Within our hearts we carry many desires. But the deepest of them all is our longing to be loved. Friendship, family, connectedness, understanding, romance, passion—there are many levels and many expressions, but all we have ever really wanted is to be loved. As Gerald May says,

> There is a desire within each of us, in the deep center of ourselves that we call our heart. We were born with it, it is never completely satisfied, and it never dies. We are often unaware of it, but it is always awake. It is the human desire for love. Every person on this earth yearns to love, to be loved, to know love. Our true identity, our reason for being, is to be found in this desire. (*The Awakened Heart*)

But because of the way our life has gone, we are, all of us, deeply ambivalent about love. This desire has caused us more pain than any other. Loneliness, isolation, misunderstanding, rejection, loss—these are the worst of our heartaches.

And that is why the offer of a life in a community of real love is the most stunning of the promises given to us about our future. To fully appreciate what promise there is for our hearts in the coming kingdom, we must grasp two things—how deeply we want love and what God has promised us in that regard.

— *Inspiration*

I've (John) been captivated by a song Jill Phillips sings called "Every Day" (on the *Jill Phillips* CD). A beautiful picture of the Great Dance we will soon be caught up in: "'Cause I could go on for a million more years if we danced like this every day."

And one of Stasi's and my favorite films is a funny Australian movie called *Strictly Ballroom*. Wait—don't dismiss it on the title. It's a great story of a young man and woman who, despite the fierce opposition of their community, follow their hearts' desire to dance "nonregulation" and win the championships. The last twenty minutes of the film are amazing, a triumph of redemption. The finale captures Yeats's poem so well—the people come together, the people come to dance, and they dance like a wave upon the sea. But you have your favorite "happy ending" films I'm sure, stories that somehow capture your heart's longing for the Feast to come (how about the end of *It's a Wonderful Life*, or *Titanic?*). You might want to visit those again as well.

SETTING FORTH

To whom did you feel special as a child? Was it a father or mother, a grandparent?

It was my (John) grandfather on my father's side. He's the only one that ever called me "Johnny," and he would always say it with such delight. I called him Pop. We were "partners." He taught me to ride, to drive a tractor, to fish with a stick and string "Huck Finn" style. I miss him dearly.

Was family a place of refuge for you as a child—a place of being *known* and *celebrated* for who you were? Is it now?

Who have been some of your good friends over the years? Name several of them here—and next to their names, jot down a few thoughts on why you enjoyed them as friends.

And do you still have those friendships now? How many good friends do you have?

When did you first "fall in love," in the sense of your first romance? What was his or her name? What was it like to fall in love?

Are you "in love" now? That is, is there someone in your life who still thrills your heart with love and romance? Would you like there to be?

Tracks of a Fellow Traveler

Romance is the deepest thing in life; it is deeper even than reality.
(G. K. Chesterton)

THE UNION THAT WE CRAVE

Is there sex in heaven?

To understand the importance of the question, you've got to recognize the ache that seems to be met only through sexual union. When God created Eve, as you will recall, he took her straight from Adam's side. None of us have fully recovered from the surgery. There is an aloneness, an *incompleteness* that we experience every day of our lives. How often do you feel deeply and truly known? Is there another soul to whom a simple glance is all that is necessary to communicate depth of understanding? Do you have someone with whom you can commune in love? This is our inconsolable longing—to know and to be known. It is our deepest ache, which we feel to be healed only in our union with another. (p. 126)

Don't rush through this question. Think about your life at home, at work, at church, with your friends—how often *do* you feel deeply and truly known?

For many, many years the answer would have been "very little." Only with a few people have I felt known—my wife, Stasi, my friends Brent and Jan and Craig.

All the rest of my relationships have been colored with a deep misunderstanding. John's too passionate, too daring, too artsy, too "feelings oriented," too focused on the heart—to name just a few of the accusations. And though my friendships are growing and my marriage is deepening, there are many days that I feel only God really understands me.

Is there another soul to whom a simple glance is all that is necessary to communicate depth of understanding? Do you have someone with whom you can commune in love?

God's design was that the two shall become one flesh. The physical oneness was meant to be the expression of a total interweaving of being. Is it any wonder that we crave this? Our alienation is removed, if only for a moment, and in the paradox of love, we are at the same time known and yet taken beyond ourselves. (p. 135)

There is no union on earth like the consummation of the love between a man and a woman. No other connection reaches as deeply as this oneness was meant to; no other passion is nearly so intense. People don't jump off bridges because they lost a grandparent. If their friend makes another friend, they don't shoot them both. Troy didn't go down in flames because somebody lost a pet. The passion that spousal love evokes is instinctive, irrational, intense, and dare I say, immortal. As the Song says,

> Love is as strong as death,
>> its jealousy unyielding as the grave.

It burns like a blazing fire,
    like a mighty flame.
Many waters cannot quench love;
    rivers cannot wash it away. (8:6–7 NIV)

Warning!

It's really important in the journey of desire to open up those rooms of longing that many of us closed long ago. As I warned in the chapter, don't let your disappointing experiences cloud your understanding of this. We have grown cynical as a society about whether intimacy is really possible. To the degree that we have abandoned soul-oneness, we have sought out merely sex, physical sex, to ease the pain. But the full union is no longer there; the orgasm comes incomplete; the heart of it has been taken away. Many have been deeply hurt. Sometimes, we must learn from what we have not known, let it teach us what *ought* to be.

Let me ask you a few questions about this deep longing. For those who are not yet married: What are you dreaming of in a lover? If your love could be all that you desire, what will that be? Have you seen it portrayed, if only in part, in one of your favorite movies? Describe it here.

And for those of you who are married, what did you once dream of in a lover? Has the reality matched the longing? If your love could become *more* of what you want, what would that be?

What are we looking for in the opposite sex?

Picture the opening sequences of the film *Last of the Mohicans*. It is 1757. England is at war with France for possession of the American colonies. "Three men, the last of a vanishing people, are on the frontier west of the Hudson River." Before us is a vast panorama of untamed wilderness. Mountain and forest as far as the eye can see. The camera takes us down into those woods, and we discover the men, running at full speed through the deep forest. Leaping across ravines, bounding with grace and speed through the heavy undergrowth, they are clearly on a great mission.

This is our first glimpse of Nathaniel, the hero of the story. Raised by the Mohawk, he is rugged, wild, *alive*. Out here on the edge of the frontier, there is something dangerous about these men. But it does not make us afraid; rather, we are all the more drawn to them. No words are spoken in this scene; no words need to be spoken. It is an image of masculinity in motion. This is what has stirred the woman's heart in Songs—to see her man's strength. And she invites that strength to come to her in the night:

> Until the day breaks
> and the shadows flee,

turn, my lover,
        and be like a gazelle
    or like a young stag
            on the rugged hills. (2:17 NIV)

There is an emptiness in the woman that only her man can fill. Is it not physically true? But it is more than just physically true. Our bodies are an outward sign of an inward reality. So, too, the woman completes her man in a uniquely beautiful way. Come to me, she says, and let your strength be fully expressed in the garden of my beauty. (p. 127)

Ladies—have I captured something here of your heart's desire? What arouses your passion for a man? Is there a picture of it in some of the men from your favorite movies? Name them, and what about them arouses you.

Come to me, she says, and let your strength be fully expressed in the garden of my beauty. Is this not the invitation that stirs a man's heart? For these are the qualities of the Beloved that captivate her Lover in the Song. He says,

How beautiful you are, my darling!
    Oh, how beautiful!
    Your eyes behind your veil are doves . . .
Your lips are like a scarlet ribbon;

> your mouth is lovely . . .
> Your two breasts are like two fawns,
> like twin fawns of a gazelle
> that browse among the lilies. (4:1, 3, 5 NIV)

Shortly after the opening sequence of the *Mohicans* in the forest, we are given our first glimpse of Cora, the heroine of the film. And such a contrast to the warriors she is. Cora is British; she wears a lovely white dress, fringed with lace and flowing to the ground. Beauty and grace have come to the frontier. She wears a summer hat with a wide brim, which for a moment veils her dark eyes, rich and deep as pools of water, soft as doves. She is mysterious, but her mystery is not one that forbids. Rather, she is captivating. Her lips are red, like the Beloved in Songs, and her fitted bodice, in no way immodest, is alluring. Though an entire war party of Hurons are not enough to trap Nathaniel, he is captured by Cora's femininity, "held captive" by her long black hair, just as the Lover is in the Song.

> My lover has gone down to his garden,
> to the beds of spices,
> to browse in the gardens
> and to gather lilies.
> I am my lover's and my lover is mine;
> he browses among the lilies. (6:2–3 NIV) (pp. 128–29)

And you men—have I captured something in what you desire of the beauty? What arouses you in a woman? Is there a picture of it in some of the women from your favorite movies? Name them, and what about them arouses you.

OUR LOVE AFFAIR WITH GOD

Small wonder that many people experience sexual passion as their highest transcendence on this earth. This love surpasses all others as the source of the world's most beautiful poetry, art, and music. Lovers reach for the stars to find words fitting enough to express what the beloved means to them and still feel those words fall short. Granted, much of it is hyperbole, expressing more the dream than the reality. But that is precisely my point. This is not merely hormones and sex drives projected outward. It is a clue to a deeper reality, a reach for something that does exist. For this exotic intimacy was given to us as a picture of something else, something truly out of this world . . . After creating this stunning portrait of a total union, the man and woman becoming one, God turns the universe on its head when he tells us that this is what *he* is seeking with *us*. (pp. 129–30)

Is that a new thought to you—that God gave us sex as a picture of something even deeper? What's your reaction to that idea?

We must look back and see the Bible for what it is—the greatest romance ever written. (p. 130)

Is that how you've understood the Bible?

Maybe this will help: the Bible uses a number of metaphors to describe our relationship to God at various stages. If you'll notice, they ascend in a stunning way:

Potter and clay. At this level we are merely aware that our lives are shaped—even broken—by a powerful hand. There isn't much communication, just the sovereignty of God at work.

Shepherd and sheep. At this stage we feel provided for, watched over, cared about. But beyond that, a sheep has little by way of true intimacy with the Shepherd. They are altogether different creatures.

Master and servant. Many, many believers are stuck in this stage, where they are committed to obey, but the relationship is mostly about receiving orders and instructions and carrying them out.

Father and child. This is certainly more intimate than being a servant; children get the run of the house, they get to climb on Daddy's lap. These fortunate souls understand God's fatherly love and care for them. They feel "at home" with God.

Friends. This stage actually opens up a deeper level of intimacy as we walk together with God, companions in a shared mission. We know what's on his heart; he knows what's on ours. There is a maturity and intimacy to the relationship.

Bridegroom and bride (lovers). Here, the words of the Song of Songs could also describe our spiritual intimacy, our union and oneness with God. Madame Guyon wrote, "I love God far more than the most affectionate lover among men loves his earthly attachment."

Where would you put your relationship with God? Why did you choose that "level"? Has it always been that way?

Does the thought of a deeper, naked intimacy with God entice you? Why . . . or why not?

It does . . . and it unnerves me. In any other relationship I can always hold a few cards close to the chest—not really and fully stand naked before them. I can retain a sense of safety and control. But with God it's different. My fig leaf feels . . . sheer. It feels SO vulnerable. Oh, how I long for a deeper intimacy with God, and yet there are hesitant places in me still. I'll draw close, taste that naked intimacy, then run from it for a while, only to return out of longing. God is gracious with me—far more than I'd be with so fickle a lover. God woos me still, and oh, how I long for the beauty of God. Dearest God, may those turnings away be less, and my stayings with you be longer.

The older Christian wedding vows contained these amazing words: "With my body, I thee worship." Maybe our forefathers weren't so prudish after all; maybe they understood sex far better than we do. To give yourself over to another, passionately and nakedly, to adore them body, soul, and spirit—we know there is something special, even sacramental about sex. It requires trust and abandonment, guided by a wholehearted devotion. What else can this be but worship? (p. 134)

Wait—before we go any farther—what *is* your idea of worship? What has been your personal experience of it?

And does a passionate Saturday night in bed with your spouse pretty much parallel your experience in the pews on Sunday morning?

I'm laughing at my own question. On the scale of naked intimacy, church feels like a postcard sent from another state.

After all, God employs explicitly sexual language to describe faithfulness (and unfaithfulness) to him. For us creatures of the flesh, sexual intimacy is the closest parallel we have to real worship. Even the world knows this. Why else would sexual ecstasy become the number one rival to communion with God? The best impostors succeed because they are nearly indistinguishable from what they are trying to imitate. We worship sex because we don't know how to worship God. But we will. Peter Kreeft writes,

> This spiritual intercourse with God is the ecstasy hinted at in all earthly intercourse, physical or spiritual. It is the ultimate reason why sexual passion is so strong, so different from other passions, so heavy with suggestions of profound meanings that just elude our grasp. (*Everything You Wanted to Know About Heaven*)

It is a mystery almost too great to mention, but God is the expression of the very thing we seek in each other. For do we not bear God's image? Are we not a living portrait of God? Indeed we are, and in a most surprising place—in our *gender* . . . God is the source of all masculine power; God is also the fountain of all feminine allure. Come to think of it, he is the wellspring of everything that has ever romanced your heart. The thundering strength of a waterfall, the delicacy of a flower, the stirring capacity of music, the richness of wine. The masculine and the feminine that fill all creation come from the same heart. What we have sought, what we have tasted in part with our earthly lovers, we will come face-to-face with in our True Love. (pp. 134–35, 136–37)

This may help the men much more than the women, but it is equally hopeful for all of us: all that you have ever longed for in the opposite sex, all that has ever turned your head or gotten your blood flowing—the real thing is to be found in God. We will "drink deeply from that fount of which we've only had a sip; to dive into that sea in which we have only waded." We'll experience true masculine strength, or true feminine allure. *Now* how do you feel about deep oneness with that Fountain of Life?

Holy smokes—when I consider that Eve is telling me something about God—that she, too, bears God's image—you betcha. I'm feeling more like Mike Mason when he says, "My wife's body is brighter and more fascinating than a flower, shier than any animal, and more breathtaking than a thousand sunsets . . . If even the image is this dazzling, what must the Original be like?" I long for the Original; to dive into that sea in which I've only waded.

THE SHARED AFFAIR

It is a manifestation of the humility of God that he creates a kingdom so rich in love that he should not be our all, but that others should be precious to us as well. Even in Eden, before the Fall, while Adam walked in Paradise with his God, even then God said, "It is not good for the man to be alone" (Gen. 2:18 NIV). He gives to us the joy of community, of family and friends to share in the Sacred Romance . . . And so our longing for intimacy reaches beyond our "one and only." We come to discover that others mean so very much to us. There is no joy like the joy of reunion because there is no sorrow like the sorrow of separation. To lose those we love and wonder if we shall ever see them again—this is our deepest grief. (p. 139)

Whom have you lost that you would you love to see again, in the life that is yet to come? Who would you hate to leave behind?

I long to see Brent again, and Pop. I pray to see my parents there, young and alive and free. Oh God, I long to know that my wife and sons will be with me. And how I long to see them all in their glory too! How incredible that will be, for us all to know each other as we really and truly were always meant to.

And are there people you would love to meet—men and women from history, maybe those you've felt a special "kinship" with? Who would you love to have a long conversation with?

I'd love to spend time with C. S. Lewis and George MacDonald, have a few beers, swap some stories. I'd love to explore the highlands with William Wallace. I'd love to get to know King David and the apostle John. Whoa . . . what a thought. They will all be there. That is just amazing. God really is "the God of the living." My mind begins to sweep through history—Shackleton, St. John of the Cross, Eric Liddle, Joshua, Moses. This is going to be very cool.

Imagine the stories that we'll hear. And all the questions that shall finally have answers. "What were you thinking when you drove the old Ford out on the ice?" "Did you hear that Betty and Dan got back together? But of course you did—you were probably involved in that, weren't you?" "How come you never told us about your time in the war?" "Did you ever know how much I loved you?" And the answers won't be one-word answers, but story after story, a feast of wonder and laughter and glad tears.

Is there someone whom you'd love to ask a question? A lost friend or family member, perhaps someone from history? What would you ask?

The setting for this will be a great party, the wedding feast of the Lamb. Now, you've got to get images of Baptist receptions entirely out of your mind—folks milling around in the church gym, holding Styrofoam cups of punch, wondering what to do with themselves. You've got to picture an Italian wedding or, better, a Jewish wedding. They roll up the rugs and push back the furniture. There is *dancing*: "Then maidens will dance and be glad, young men and old as well" (Jer. 31:13 NIV). There is *feasting*: "On this mountain the LORD Almighty will prepare a feast of rich food for all peoples" (Isa. 25:6 NIV). Can you imagine what kind of cook God must be?) And there is *drinking*— the feast God says he is preparing includes "a banquet of aged wine—the best of meats and the finest of wines." In fact, at his Last Supper our Bridegroom said he will not drink of "the fruit of the vine until the kingdom of God comes" (Luke 22:18 NIV). Then he'll pop a cork. (pp. 141–42)

Think of some of the best celebrations you've had in your life—great birthdays or Christmases, reunions, intimate dates. Describe a few of them.

The Ritz Carlton Laguna Beach is one of the most luxurious hotels in southern California. Nestled on a bluff above its private cove with white sandy beach, the hotel exudes romance. Its Mediterranean architecture lifts the Ritz out of space and time, creating a fairy-tale ambience. Arches and tile walkways lead to fountain courtyards and terraces with breathtaking views of the Pacific. The tropical climate nourishes a lush canopy of purple and red bougainvillea, whimsical flower gardens, rich green lawns, and swaying palms. Staying at the Ritz, one can almost forget, if for a moment, that the Fall ever happened. Stasi and I enjoyed a weekend of escape there thanks to a business conference I was asked to attend.

Late one evening I slipped away from the meeting to wander the grounds alone. I felt restless inside and thought a walk might be calming. Something drew me through the terraces toward the ocean. As I wandered over the beautifully manicured lawns, more luxuriant than any carpet, the sounds of music and laughter from parties inside mingled with the scent of the flower beds in the warm ocean breeze. My restlessness grew. Standing on the edge of the cliff with the crashing of the waves below and the shining of the stars above, I felt the restlessness swell into an ache. As Simone Weil said, there are only two things that pierce the human heart: beauty and affliction. I was run clean-through by the beauty of it all, overcome by an ache for a home I have never seen. (John, in The Sacred Romance)

Have you ever danced with abandon, with freedom and joy? When?

Tracks of a Fellow Traveler

Now I am living a dream.
I can't believe, can't believe we are here . . .
'Cause I could go on for a million more years
If we danced like this every day.
("Every Day," on the Jill Phillips CD, by Andy Gullahorn and Jill Phillips, 1998)

And have you ever enjoyed a really great feast? What have been some of your best memories of dining and drinking with loved ones—and what was the effect on your heart?

To one group of his day, who believed that "physical death" was the cessation of the individual's existence, Jesus said, "God is not the God of the dead, but of the living" (Luke 20:38). His meaning was that those who love and are loved by God are not allowed to cease to exist, because they are God's treasures. He delights in them and intends to hold onto them. He has even prepared for them an individualized eternal work in his vast universe. (*The Divine Conspiracy*)

I'll say more about that work in the next chapter. What is vital for us to grasp now, Willard says, is simply this: *"The life we now have as the persons we now are will continue in the universe in which we now exist."* (p. 140)

So, it would be good to begin to make some plans for that life and those relationships. Who would you love to spend time with—and what would you love to do together? Take music lessons from Bach? Learn archery from King David? Ask C. S. Lewis for a few more stories from Narnia?

Tracks of a Fellow Traveler

All mankind is of one author, and is one volume; when one man dies, one chapter is not torn out of the book, but translated into a better language; and every chapter must be so translated; God employs several translators: some pieces are translated by age, some by sickness, some by war, some by justice; but God's hand is in every translation; and his hand shall bind up all our scattered leaves again, for that library where every book shall open to one another. (John Donne)

What hopes has this chapter raised in your heart?

And what does that free you to do with the days ahead of you now?

Write out your prayer this chapter has inspired.

THE ADVENTURE BEGINS

And in the perfect time, O perfect God,
When we are in our home, our natal home,
When joy shall carry every sacred load,
And from its life and peace no heart shall roam,
What if thou make us able to make like thee—
To light with moons, to clothe with greenery,
To hang gold sunsets o'er a rose and purple sea!
—GEORGE MACDONALD

Enter into the joy of your master.
—JESUS OF NAZARETH

— Counsel for the Journey

There is one more aspect of our future we must explore if we are to recover heart for the journey of our lives. For though it will be unspeakable joy to live forever in a fully restored universe with the company of the truly intimate, it is not enough. There is something core to our beings and set within our deepest desires that remains untouched. For as the nineteenth-century preacher Thomas Chalmers wrote, one of the "Grand Essentials" of human happiness is having something to do.

Think again about the three great longings of your heart, those deep desires for Beauty, Intimacy, and Adventure. Is your life to come going to involve adventure? If not, how could you be happy there? What about all those gifts and abilities God has placed within you—do those have a future?

Not only is it essential, if we are to live with hope, to know that our future life will be full of creative work and all sorts of adventures, this truth also puts our present life into a whole new light. We are in Training, and a remarkable

Promotion is about to be ours. So come and explore more than you ever have: What is it you would love to *do?*

— *Inspiration*

There's a marvelous song by Carolyn Arends called "Seize the Day," which more than any other captures what it means to live from our hearts in our true design. I (Craig) prefer the live version from the *Seize the Day & Other Stories* CD (2000).

SETTING FORTH

Some people love what they do. They are the fortunate souls, who have found a way to link what they are truly gifted at (and therefore what brings them joy) with a means of paying the bills. But most of the world merely toils to survive, and no one gets to use his gifts all the time. On top of that, there is the curse of thorns and thistles, the futility that tinges all human efforts at the moment. As a result, we've come to think of work as a result of the Fall. You can see our cynicism in the fact that we've chosen the cartoon character Dilbert as the icon of our working days. His is a hopeless life of futility and anonymity in the bowels of a large corporation. We don't even know what he does—only that it's meaningless. We identify with him, feeling at some deep level the apparent futility of our lives. (p. 155)

Let's start with your life right now—do you love what you do for a living? Why . . . or why not?

How are the hours of your days actually spent? Be specific—what is it you actually do 8 to 5? What tasks are you performing?

Do you feel your gifts are being fully used? Do those tasks call out all the potential God set within you?

> NO. NO. It seems that I (Craig) am limited (in my work/ministry context) to four cylinders when I have eight to offer. Time passes, things change, I've grown . . . there's a restlessness to be a part of something different, very different . . . to be somewhere more spacious . . . to exhaust myself in a labor and freedom that require all of me.

Is what you're doing now the thing you dreamed of doing when you were a child? What were your dreams for your life's work?

If you could land your "dream job," what would it be?

Our creative nature is essential to who we are as human beings—as image bearers—and it brings us great joy to live it out with freedom and skill. Even if it's a simple act such as working on your photo albums or puttering in the garden—these, too, are how we have a taste of what was meant to rule over a small part of God's great kingdom. (p. 154)

What do you love to do with your free time? Do you have any hobbies—or are there hobbies you'd love to get to but just haven't had time? Whatever that is for you—gardening or working in the shop or antique collecting—what about it makes it something you love?

Though it will be unspeakable joy to live forever in a fully restored universe with the company of the truly intimate, it is not enough. (p. 145)

Does this statement surprise you, perhaps even sound heretical, or do you find yourself saying, "Yes!"? Are you aware of a desire that yearns for more than to live forever in beauty and intimacy . . . but doing nothing at all? Why wouldn't that be enough for you?

Tracks of a Fellow Traveler

We need to remember that the whole nature of man is redeemed and shall be up in glory. Man consists not only of spirit but also of body and soul. He owns a personality, possesses a will, desires, capacity to love and be loved . . . When we realize that the whole being of man is saved—body, soul and spirit . . . we realize then how the heavenly bliss must be a place where all our capacities for life will gain fruition and development. Thus it comes about that we must have something more in heaven than "going to church." There must be all the things necessary for a full and complete existence. (N. A. Woychuk, Life in Heaven)

I think the fear of being bored is an unspoken fear of many people about the life that is coming. After all, the never-ending sing-along in the sky isn't exactly breathtaking. Spending a weekend at the beach beats that hands down. (pp. 145–46)

Set all your doctrine and presuppositions aside for a moment. What would you love to do with your eternal life?

We've somehow overlooked a line in the parable of the talents, a single sentence that speaks volumes about the connection between our present and future life. As you'll recall, the landowner in the story has been away on a journey. In the parallel version told in Luke, the parable of the minas, he is a man of "noble birth" who has gone to "a distant country to have himself appointed king" (19:11–27 NIV). Upon his return, he rewards those faithful members of his staff in a way that at first seems, well, like no reward at all. "You have been faithful with a few things; I will put you in charge of many things." Luke's version has it this way: "Because you have been trustworthy in a very small matter, take charge of ten cities." This is their bonus—more to do? Wouldn't a vacation make a better reward? My boys clean their rooms so they can go out and play, not so they can clean the rest of the house. Yet Jesus thinks that he is sharing something delightful with us. The landowner then says, "Come and share your master's happiness." Or, as the King James has it, "Enter into the joy of thy lord." To understand what he means, we must have a closer look at God's joyful activity and our inherent design. (p. 146)

What thoughts have you had about God as a rewarder? What kind of a reward do you anticipate? What stirs in your heart with questions such as this? Excitement? Fear? Guilt/shame? Anxiety? Adoration? Hope? Has it felt like a "reward" or something else?

I don't know that I've ever, in the past, had a confidence that a good reward awaits me. The ever-deepening questions, "Is God really good?"; "Is there really grace extended to me?" are so tied into how I live my life and evaluate it. My performance and shame orientation wouldn't allow me to accept that I might be rewarded for anything . . . that's changing. Praise God!

THE JOY OF THE MASTER

How marvelous it is to watch a master artist at work. We [Stasi and I] enjoyed a wonderful performance of Chausson's *Poeme for Violin and Orchestra* last night. The young woman who played the lead violin was simply beautiful in her long white gown, her graceful arms working the bow and strings with finesse. It was a joy just to watch her play. And the *Poeme* itself is an enchanting piece of music, almost ethereal. It fit her and the mood of the summer evening perfectly. And so it was with one accord that the audience rose in applause at the close of the performance. (pp. 146–47)

Can you recall being captured by a performance or work of a master—someone who is really, really good at what he or she does? Who, when, where . . . what captivated you? Describe it.

Is there an opportunity for you to enjoy a master artist in your community soon? Perhaps attending a concert, visiting a museum or art gallery, enjoying a dance performance? Consider going and then writing about your experience. For now, list a number of your favorite pieces of music, musicians, athletes, teams, artists, art pieces, architecture, poetry, craftsmanship.

Take time to enjoy some of these "favorites," as you can, this week. Describe what it is you enjoy about these favorites.

Do you see yourself as a creative person? Would people know you to be creative? How is creativity viewed in your circle?

I find myself hesitant to accept fully what others say of me . . . that I am creative. I've always had an eye for aesthetics, enjoying the creativity of others as well as creating something beautiful. For years, most of my Christian life, those parts of my heart were buried. I began college as an art major; I loved graphic arts, ink and pencil drawing and watercolors, and dreamed of creating a line of greeting cards . . . drawing, painting were a defining part of my life. I became a Christian at twenty-one and assimilated into a community that, without ever saying so, devalued individuality and the personal uniqueness of our gifts, passions, and talents. Thus, something very true to me was smothered and eventually died. Aesthetics, art, creativity, and for that matter any passion outside the Great Commission was viewed as a compromise to "carnal" pursuits (again, these things are never said with words . . . but the Christian culture I'm very familiar with "said" it in other ways). This is an area of my soul God is restoring.

As creation was unfolding from the hands of the Master, like wet clay on a potter's wheel, a great ovation erupted: "The morning stars sang together and all the angels shouted for joy" (Job 38:7 NIV). But of course. He has just finished sculpting the islands of Greece so that their white sandy beaches perfectly rim those azure seas. Then he watered the jungles of Malaysia to sustain an exotic array of orchids, after which he painted sunsets over the Sahara and hurled the Himalayas upward, treacherous peaks scraping the roof of the world.

And he doesn't stop there. Into this breathtaking setting of a thousand different habitats God places "the fish of the sea and the birds of the air . . . every living creature that moves on the ground" (Gen. 1:28 NIV). Chameleons and caribou, porcupines and porpoises. How do we begin to describe this God whose image we bear? *Artistic* is the only word that even comes close. *Powerful, awesome, majestic*—yet *intricate, delicate, whimsical. Creative*, without a doubt. (p. 147)

From your travels or the travels of others (Discovery Channel, Travel Channel), or perhaps from photographic magazines (like *National Geographic* or coffee-table photo books), what of God's creation strikes you as stunning in its beauty, intricacy, design? What of God's artistry brings you to your feet in appreciative applause?

Living at the beach, I've applauded a fair number of God's awesome sunsets over the water, and am always on the watch for another one. Most recently the subtle give-and-take saga of an ocean's shoreline has captured my attention. The rhythm of the tidal zone's life: rocks versus waves, the tidal pool fiefdoms, the humorous sprinting back and forth of the sandpipers, the gull regiments lined together facing the wind, the changing contours, textures, and colors of the and . . . The other day God orchestrated a dolphin show better than Sea World. About a dozen dolphins were riding waves, jumping in pairs, doing flips, splashing, frolicking in the surf. As you watched you had to join in their laughter.

And that was just the beginning. Although God rested on the seventh day, he hasn't been lying around ever since. Jesus said, "My Father is always at his work to this very day, and I, too, am working" (John 5:17 NIV). For many people this is a new thought—that God is still quite active. Life has led them to believe that he may have gotten things off to a great start, but then he left on vacation or perhaps went to attend to more important matters. But the creative overture recorded in Genesis was only the first movement of a great symphony that has been swelling ever since. The opening notes were not *staccato,* but sustenuto, ongoing, unfolding. He's not just sitting around on a throne somewhere. (pp. 147–48)

What have you viewed God as doing with all his "time"? Is this thought of God *still* working new to you?

I'm cracking up at how little I've thought about some of these issues. This is "a new thought." Yes, I assumed God was busy, but not that busy . . . He's God, right? I think I was a bit of a deist . . . God set creation in motion, then leaned back on a sofa and watched it all unfold. I've never really given much time or thought to what God is doing. Pondering that a bit exposes how I've viewed God as a bit distant, uninvolved to some degree . . .

The only way to describe his ongoing creative activity is *extravagant* . . . You don't suppose he experiences his part in running the universe as drudgery, do you? Did Margot Fonteyn and Rudolf Nureyev love to dance? Does Michael Jordon love to play basketball? So God loves his work. He isn't ashamed to call it all "very good" . . . Dallas Willard notes,

> We should, to begin with, think that God leads a very interesting life, and that he is full of joy. Undoubtedly he is the most joyous being in the universe. The abundance of his love and generosity is inseparable from his infinite joy. All of the good and beautiful things from which we occasionally drink tiny droplets of soul-exhilarating joy, God continuously experiences in all their breadth and depth . . . We are enraptured by a well-done movie sequence or by a few bars from an opera or lines from a poem. We treasure our great experiences for a lifetime, and we may have very few of them. But he is simply one great inexhaustible and eternal experience of all that is good and true and beautiful and right. This is what we must think of when we hear theologians and philosophers speak of him as a perfect being. *This is his life. (The Divine Conspiracy)*

And it is *this* life, with all its joyful creativity and power and unending happiness, that he says he is going to share with us. This is "the joy of your master" that we are to be welcomed into. It rather beats harps and halos, wouldn't you say? For we long to find our place in the world, caring for and developing creation in all its diverse potential. It is this for which we were made. (pp. 148–49, 150)

What does it stir in your heart to anticipate a life like that?

LITTLE GODS

"So God created man in his own image, in the image of God he created him; male and female he created them." Thus is humanity trumpeted onto the scene, in verse 27 of the first chapter of Genesis (NIV). It is a passage familiar to most of us. Too familiar perhaps, for we rarely wonder about what it means. Right here, at the beginning of our existence, is the single phrase our Creator uses to characterize us, and most of us haven't the foggiest idea what it implies. (p. 151)

Though you may have thought of this before, write out what it means for you to be an image bearer.

More often than not we think of godliness in moral terms. When we hear that so-and-so is a "godly person," we assume that he is devout, or perhaps self-sacrificing, and certainly more virtuous than most. But when Genesis declares we are God's image, it is describing not certain qualities of our character but *capacities of our nature* . . . In other words, we are *made* like God in our creative powers because we are to *be* like God in ruling the earth . . . Our original design was for a life of creative rule, to share in the overall care and development of God's creation. The poet writes because she is made in God's image; the builder loves to build for the same reason. Entrepreneurs risk capital ventures, baseball players go to the batting cages, and cooks experiment with spices all for the same reason. It is what we *are*. (pp. 151–52)

Can you see that image at work in your life? What do you long to build or repair, to uncover or design, to nurture or care for?

Is the thought of having some special work to do in heaven growing on you? Are your thoughts enlarging about what you'll actually do in heaven—that is, in the coming kingdom of God?

What's fairly new is giving thought to heaven! It's amazing really, how long I've gone in my Christian journey without being drawn into many conversations regarding heaven. My thoughts about heaven have been quite simple, generic . . . it's good, it's long . . . I'll be enthralled in the presence of God . . . and that's been about it. Yes, the thought of having a task, a role, or a part in the ongoingness of heaven is new. My initial concern is that my task would be perfunctory, not really a fit to my desires, my identity (some low-level entry position) . . . I'd hate to be in a heavenly widget factory. In some ways my lack of thought regarding heaven is a reflection of where my focus has been. For most of my life, all my desires were viewed as capable of being filled here on earth (such small desires); heaven really held nothing for me, other than the best alternative to hell.

ON MOZART AND MARTHA STEWART

This is precisely what happens when God shares with mankind his own artistic capacity and then sets us down in a paradise of unlimited potential. It is an act of creative *invitation*, like providing Monet with a studio for the summer, stocked full of brushes and oils and empty canvases. Or like giving Mozart full use of an orchestra and a concert hall for an autumn of composing. Or like setting Martha Stewart loose in a gourmet kitchen on a snowy winter weekend, just before the holidays. You needn't provide instructions or motivation; all you have to do is release them to be who they are, and remarkable things will result. As the poet Hopkins wrote, "What I do is me: for that I came."

Oh, how we long for this—for a great endeavor that draws upon our every faculty, a great "life's work" that we could throw ourselves into. (p. 153)

What would others say your current life's work is—what at this point in time is your legacy?

To what degree and where does your life reflect the fact that you are a creative ruler over a dominion?

It's easy to live from an inadequate understanding of what it means to be a "ruler" . . . I've seen and been guilty of the abuse of position and power. I've also made a career out of being passive (though it's never been blatantly obvious). I want nothing to do with either of those models of ruling. My life now seems to be moving in good directions. My desires seem to be more truly concerned with God's plan for others versus my demands of others. I find myself living in the larger story more now, though it still seems very new to me, too new, actually. Several of the "dominions" in which I reflect this creative-ruler dimension of God are: my family (what sway I have over the hearts of my wife and daughters); in my church (Oh, dear Lord, may I, in words and actions, be used to see hearts set free by the beauty and the power of the gospel); among my friends (to love, allow them to love, to share in all the mystery, beauty, and adventures of life together . . . enjoying an authentic communion and God's people). I've lived, and still battle living, in smaller stories. I'm not joking when I say . . . some of the dominions I've ruled over are keeping the garage organized and the spice rack alphabetized.

Even if we are loved, it is not enough. We yearn to be *fruitful*, to do something of meaning and value that flows naturally out of the gifts and capacities of our souls. But of course—we were meant to be the kings and queens of the earth.

Dorothy Sayers once wrote, "Work is not, primarily, a thing one does to live, but the thing one lives to do." If only it were so; if only we could land our "dream job," where we'd be paid to do what we love. (p. 155)

Now, having done the past few pages of journaling, give some more thought to what your dream job here and now would be. After all, you are in training now to rule as you will then. It's time to get on with your life's true calling. What is it? And what could possibly keep you from chasing it?

Tracks of a Fellow Traveler

Twenty years invested in a professional practice as a attorney that was safe, secure, prestigious. With ten to twelve years left in professional practice, a question begins to surface, a new question: "How do I want to spend those years?" A new category emerges in making such a huge personal decision, "What do I _want_ to do?" Now the thought of continuing to do what I've done for twenty years seems rather mundane. I began to ask myself, "Do I want to pursue another vision for something other than the status quo?" I began to listen to my desire—a desire for something more, a challenge to use parts of me that hadn't been used in a more demanding environment—in the courtroom. More adventure, a battle, a fight . . . and oh, by the way, are you good enough to be with the stallions? Or are you going to be content with the geldings back at the gristmill?

The options are gone. I changed my career. And I'm loving it. (Bill)

THE MONARCHY RESTORED

Let's come back for a moment to the restoration of the earth. In Romans 8 (NIV), Paul says something outrageous. He says that all our sufferings are "not worth comparing" with the glory that will be revealed in us. It seems hard to believe, given the way life can break your heart. The human race has seen an unspeakable amount of suffering. What can possibly make that seem like nothing? "The glory that will be revealed in us" (8:18). The Great Restoration. Paul then goes on to say, "The creation waits in eager expectation for the sons of God to be revealed" (8:19). The release of a fully restored creation is being more or less held back, waiting upon *our* restoration. Why? Because only then can we handle it. Only when we ourselves have been restored can we take our place again as the kings and queens of creation. Or did you not know? The day is coming when Christ will appoint you as one of his regents over his great and beautiful universe. This has been his plan all along. (p. 156)

Did you know that God had a plan for your life that involved more than singing his praises forever?

Christ is not joking when he says that we shall inherit the kingdom prepared for us and shall reign with him forever. We will take the position for which we have been uniquely made and will rule *as he does*—meaning with creativity and power . . .

Much of the activity of God in our lives is bringing us to the place where he can entrust us with this kind of influence. God takes our training so seriously because he fully intends to promote us. Will it be joy? Does Stephen Hawking enjoy physics? Does Mark McGwire enjoy hitting it out of the park? There are so many ways this "reigning" will be expressed—as unique and varied as there are human souls. God has quite a few "possessions," and it's going to take a lot of looking after by men and women uniquely fitted for the task. (pp. 157, 158)

With this new perspective in mind—that God is training you, preparing you for a big promotion—can you begin to see his hand behind the drama of your life? Can you see something of the preparation? Where—in what jobs, assignments, events?

Would it have any impact on your life to know now—at least in a "sense"—what you'll be doing in heaven?

What immediately strikes me is, "I'm not sure it would have an impact." Given a bit more thought, it seems the impact would be a freeing, joyous hope-expectation. So many hopes and dreams, aspirations and desires of my heart for life, relationships, adventure, intimacy, and impact will by and large be partially fulfilled at best. Many unfulfilled. To know that heaven will include the fulfillment of deep desires God has written upon my heart gives me hope, an expectation of being and doing things there I never could here . . . that's good! There's less pressure to grab all the gusto you can now (because all you have is now), knowing there's another chapter to this story.

THE GLORIOUS FREEDOM

"Life," as a popular saying goes, "is not a dress rehearsal. Live it to the fullest." What a setup for a loss of heart. No one gets all he desires; no one even comes close.

If this is it, we are lost. But what if life is a dress rehearsal? What if the real production is about to begin? As C. S. Lewis wrote,

> The miracles that have already happened are, of course, as the Scripture often says, the first fruits of that cosmic summer which is presently coming on. Christ has risen, and so we shall rise. St. Peter or a few seconds walked on the water; and the day will come when there will be a remade universe, infinitely obedient to the will of glorified and obedient men, when we can do all things, when we shall be those gods that we are described as being in Scripture. *(The Grand Miracle)*
> (pp. 158–59, 160)

Write out the prayer your heart is stirred to at this point.

ENTERING MORE DEEPLY INTO DESIRE

Blessed are those who hunger and thirst.
—JESUS OF NAZARETH

And in me wake hope, fear, boundless desire.
—GEORGE MacDONALD

― *Counsel for the Journey*

I (John) hope that by now you see why I have spent three chapters trying to bring eternity out of the clouds and into our conscious lives. The dilemma of desire is the deepest dilemma we will ever face. Its dangers are deep and potentially fatal. How, then, shall we not lose heart? If we manage to somehow hang on to our desire, how do we keep from being consumed by it? The secret is known to all of us, though we may have forgotten that we know it. Who wants to fill up with snacks on Thanksgiving Day? Who goes out to buy presents for themselves on Christmas Eve? Is there anyone in his right mind who looked for someone to date at his wedding rehearsal? When we are convinced that something delicious is about to be ours, we are free to live in expectation, and it draws us on in anticipation.

To find the Land of Desire, you must take the Journey of Desire. You can't get there by any other means. If we are to take up the trail and get on with our quest, we've got to get our hearts back . . . which means getting our desire back. And so in this leg of the journey you are seeking a deeper knowledge and understanding of your desire; you are moving *forward* by moving *inward*.

— *Inspiration*

Our friend the sea lion is about to undergo a sort of transformation, a resolve of desire that sets him on his way toward his true home. There is a very powerful picture of the intense power and resolve of desire at the end of the film *The Truman Show*. Truman is a man who's been trapped his whole life in an artificial world—artificial friends, artificial family, artificial job. He tries a time or two to escape but is thwarted by the powers that hold him back. Finally, he faces his deepest fear—water—climbs aboard a sailboat, and heads out to find the love of his dreams. Even when a fierce storm capsizes him, he does not give in. The last twenty minutes of this movie are very powerful.

Three weeks after the wind ceased to blow, the sea lion had a dream. Now, as I told you before, there were other nights in which he had dreamed of the sea. But those were long ago and nearly forgotten. Even still, the ocean that filled his dreams this night was so beautiful and clear, so vast and deep, it was as if he were seeing it for the very first time. The sunlight glittered on its surface, and as he dived, the waters all around him shone like an emerald. If he swam quite deep, it turned to jade, cool and dark and mysterious. But he was never frightened, not at all. For I must tell you that in all his dreams of the sea, he had never before found himself in the company of other sea lions. This night there were many, round about him, diving and turning, spinning and twirling. They were playing.

Oh, how he hated to wake from that wonderful dream. The tears running down his face were the first wet thing he had felt in three weeks. But he did not pause even to wipe them away; he did not pause, in fact, for anything at all. He set his face to the east, and he began to walk as best a sea lion can.

"Where are you going?" asked the tortoise.

"I am going to find the sea."

What has happened in the sea lion's heart? What's driving him now?

Have you ever felt that kind of resolve? What stirred it?

SETTING FORTH

When I can no more stir my soul to move,
And life is but the ashes of a fire;
When I can but remember that my heart
Once used to live and love, long and aspire—
Oh, be thou then the first, the one thou art;
Be thou the calling, before all answering love,
And in me wake hope, fear, boundless desire. (George MacDonald, *Diary of an Old Soul*)

Why would MacDonald (writing toward the end of his life, by the way, and not as a reckless young man) pray something as seemingly crazy as this? Do you understand his plea better now?

There are three things that we must come to terms with in our deep heart. First, we must have life. Second, we cannot arrange for it. Third, it is coming. Now we are ready to proceed on our way. (p. 164)

Over the years of your journey, God will take you back through deeper cycles of learning each of these three "essentials." But for now, how clear are you on each core truth? Are you more deeply aware now how you were made for *life*, and nothing less will do? Are you also aware that despite your best efforts, you cannot arrange for the life you need? And finally, is there a real and growing conviction in your heart that it is coming, life *is* coming to you?

BATTLE AND JOURNEY

Life is now a battle and a journey. As Eugene Peterson reminds us, "We must fight the forces that oppose our becoming whole; we must find our way through difficult and unfamiliar territory to our true home." It's not that there aren't joy and beauty, love and adventure now—there are. The invasion of the kingdom has begun. But life in its fullness has yet to come. So we must take seriously the care of our hearts. We must watch over our desire with a fierce love and vigilance, as if we were protecting our most precious possession. (p. 164)

Is that how you think about your heart these days—as your most precious possession? Does the way you live reflect that conviction?

More and more it is, thank God. Just the other night I (John) was really feeling the pressure to get this project done, finish this journal. But I'd been working on it all day, and my heart was tired. I simply walked away from it, went upstairs, played with my boys for a while, enjoyed dinner with the family, and even then I didn't go back and devote the evening to it. Oh, I felt the demand nagging at me, the strong pull to just go and write, regardless of my weary heart. But I saw it for what it was; I knew the damage it would do. It was good to say no.

So let me say it again: life is now a battle and a journey. This is the truest explanation for what is going on, the only way to rightly understand our experience. Life is not a game of striving and indulgence. It is not a long march of duty and obligation. It is not, as Henry Ford once said, "one damn thing after another." Life is a desperate quest through dangerous country to a destination that is, beyond all our wildest hopes, indescribably good. Only by conceiving of our days in this manner can we find our way safely through. (p. 164)

Is that how you've conceived of life—as a "desperate quest through dangerous country to a destination that is, beyond all our wildest hopes, indescribably good"? How *have* you thought of life?

Have your convictions about life changed through this journey?

RECOVERING DESIRE

I continue to be stunned by the level of deadness that most people consider normal and seem to be contented to live with. (p. 165)

As you've been going through this journal, has anything changed in the way you see the people around you—your family, friends, coworkers, fellow churchgoers? As you've experienced your desire growing, what have you noticed about theirs?

And, how have they responded to you and your journey of desire?

It seems that the dividing lines are becoming more and more clear—jealousy (masked as criticism, anger, or suspicion) and yearning. The more I walk the journey I must walk, the more I understand what Jesus meant when he said that some people will want to kill you and they'll think they are serving God. Oh, they won't say it so openly; what they'd rather do is "kill" my reputation, or raise "theological concerns," but what they're really doing is reacting with fear to their own hearts' inner stirrings, which they've tried so hard to push down for so many years.

Happily, on the other hand, there is the Fellowship of the Heart—those thirsty souls who know real life when they see it; they want freedom and a true walk with God, and they are willing more and more to take the risk. Some of them have become my precious allies.

Tracks of a Fellow Traveler

The New Testament has lots to say about self-denial, but not about self-denial as an end in itself. We are told to deny ourselves and take up our crosses in order that we may follow Christ; and nearly every description of what we shall ultimately find if we do so contains an appeal to desire . . . Indeed, if we consider the unblushing promises of reward and the staggering nature of the rewards promised in the Gospels, it would seem that Our Lord finds our desires not too strong, but too weak. We are half-hearted creatures, fooling about with drink and sex and ambition, when infinite joy is offered us, like an ignorant child who wants to go on making mud pies in a slum because he cannot imagine what is meant by the offer of a holiday at the sea. We are far too easily pleased. (C. S. Lewis, The Weight of Glory)

If only it were as strong as drink and sex and ambition. We've been bought off by clean socks and television. We'll sell our birthright for a little bit of pleasure and some peace and quiet. I understand. It hasn't taken us long to realize that life is not going to offer what we truly want, and so we've learned to reduce our desires to a more manageable size. (p. 166)

And thinking a bit more about the people in your world, what have they been bought off by? Can you be specific? Name the people that come to mind and what they've settled for.

Now, closer to home—do you think that Jesus considers *your* desires too strong, or too weak? Why do you say that?

OUR DEEPEST HEART

Many committed Christians are wary about getting in touch with their desires, not because they want to settle for less, but because they fear that they will discover some dark hunger lurking in their hearts. As I've said, the father of lies takes many people out of the battle and ends their journey by keeping them in the shallows of their desire, tossing them a bone of pleasure, and thus convincing them that they are satisfied. However, once we begin to move from that place, his strategy changes. He threatens us from going into the deep waters by telling us that our core desires are evil. (pp. 166–67)

"Your desires are bad. You ought to be ashamed of that. You should be thinking about others." How has the enemy whispered to you that your desires are bad? One example might be a perfectly good desire that you feel bad for having. Another might be a desire for something you know is wrong, but it never occurred to you that it might not be your real desire at all.

> Oh yes, I know both . . . well. My yearning to have some horses, to ride the open ranges with my wife and sons. I feel stupid for wanting that. It seems extravagant, way outside what I should be focused on. And yes, many times Satan has lied to me about what I really want. He'll suggest a temptation to my mind—then accuse me for having it cross my mind.

For those who have been born of the Spirit and become new creatures in Christ, sin is no longer the truest thing about us. Since the coming of Christ, everything has changed. The joy of the new covenant is the transformation of our deepest being. As Christians, we have a new heart, and that means nothing less than this: our core desires are good. "I will put my law in their minds and write it on their hearts" (Jer. 31:33 NIV). We don't need to fear recovering our desire because our desire is from God and for God. That is what is most true about us. (p. 168)

The entire future of your Christian life hangs on this promise that you've been given a new heart. Do you believe it? Why . . . or why not?

Yes, we still struggle with sin, with our tendency to kill desire or give our hearts over to false desires. But that is not who and what we truly are. If we really believe the New Covenant, we'll be able to embrace our desire. So, let's come back to the simple question Jesus asks of us all: What do you want? Don't minimize it; don't try to make sure it sounds spiritual; don't worry about whether or not you can obtain it. Just stay with the question until you begin to get an answer. This is the way we keep current with our hearts. (p. 168)

What do you want . . .
In your relationships?

In your work?

In your play?

With God?

WHAT DO YOU WANT?

"It's hard to be holy and passionate." Cindy sighed as she said this. A bright young woman and a sincerely committed follower of Christ, she's also a bit more vulnerable to men than she'd like to be. It seems that the only way Cindy can keep from chasing after physical intimacy with a man is to bury herself in grad school. But as I've said earlier, the "run from desire" approach never works, and she soon finds herself leaving the books for another compromising situation. "Why can't I get beyond this?" she asked. "I'm praying and reading my Bible every day. But still I fall." "What are you looking for?" I asked in return. We sat in silence for a few minutes. "I really don't know." "That's your problem . . . you don't know. And so your unexamined desires rule you." After a few moments she asked, "Is it pleasure? Excitement?" She was clueless. As intelligent as Cindy is, I wasn't surprised that she had no clue as to why she couldn't break her addiction to men. As a rule, most of us live far from our hearts. We need to be much more acquainted with them. We need to know what we want. (pp. 168–69)

As Cindy and I continued to talk about her life, what surfaced was her desperate desire to be loved. She never really felt loved by her father. Her craving to be deeply loved is good—she's just been taking it in wrong directions. How about you? Now take a struggle area in your life—a desire that keeps getting you in trouble, or threatening to. Can you see the desire *beneath* the desire? What I mean is, separate what you are desiring from the object you think will provide it.

The path to a clearer knowledge of our desire depends on how we've been handling it. Those who have buried desire beneath years of duty and obligation may need to give all that a rest so that their hearts can come to the surface. Abandon all but the most essential duties for a while. You still have to pay the bills, but everything you can jettison, you should. Do nothing unless it reflects your true desire. (p. 169)

Those of you living in the duty camp—what can you give up? The idea might seem impossible or crazy at first. Objections rush to your mind. Your immediate response might be, "Nothing. I don't dare set any of this down." Do you see how bound you are to duty?! We're talking about the survival of your heart here. Of course, you will have to trust God . . . deeply. Let somebody else carry the weight for a while. Or just let it crash. For how long? More than a week. I gave up church for a year. If that sounds too crazy, then how about a three-month break? What will it be?

Those who have been living to indulge desire will need to give that a rest too. What does your heart feel when I suggest you give up your obsession? Listen to the panic—there's something beneath it, something you need to know. Now, I understand that going cold turkey may seem overwhelming, unattainable. You may have tried that before and failed. Let me offer a more gentle approach. Simply stay in your desire for fifteen minutes longer than you usually do. When you're feeling a pull to the refrigerator or the gym or the bedroom, stop and let the desire just be; let it become more acute. Don't do anything with it. Let yourself feel it, and as you do, let your heart put some honest words to what you're feeling. You might be surprised what you find there. (pp. 169–70)

Yes . . . set it down for a while. I'm talking about those desires that seem perfectly innocent—your routine of watching TV, or going shopping, or playing golf. Take a break from your comforters and let the deeper issues of your heart show up. What is the comforter you are willing to give up for awhile?

This . . . involves the hidden places of your heart, which are almost always revealed in your desire. But few of us take the time to look at the desire *beneath* the desire. A friend just spent thousands of dollars to undo a previous operation that tied her fallopian tubes. She wants to have another baby; no, she *needs* to have another baby. It has nothing to do with a baby. This is where she experiences being needed and wanted and loved. How many woman derive their sense of self from their children? On and on it goes. Do we purchase a new home merely for more space, or does it mean security to us? We seek a better job. Might we be seeking a sense of identity, of being a successful person? It's not that the longing roused by any of these things is wrong. It's that we must learn what is actually *being* roused. The more attuned we are to our true desire, the less prone we'll be to impostors. (pp. 170–71)

As you set down the duty or the indulgence, *pay attention.* What begins to surface in your heart?

TEMPTATION

We can learn many things about the journey of desire in the story of Jesus' wilderness trial . . . The first thing we learn is that we're going to hunger. It's normal; expect it. Jesus' hunger validates my own. I needn't be embarrassed by it, try to hide it, or diminish it in some way. Sometimes we feel guilty about the depth of our desire, and we end up repenting of the wrong thing.

The devil sees his opportune moment. He came to Jesus as he comes to us—in our hunger. And what he says is simply this: "You don't have to stay hungry, you know. There are options." He's not lying at this point; there usually are options. There is often something we can do about our hunger, and the options increase the more we are willing to turn away from trusting God. (pp. 171–72)

What "options" has the devil presented to you in the past week or two?

I know exactly what it is: busyness. Just get really busy, John, and you won't have to face the emptiness and hunger that you're feeling right now. Get busy with good things, ministry even. Bury your heart beneath a deluge of activity. Neglect it; put it aside. Wouldn't it be easier?

The lie is that the options will bring us what we most deeply want and need. They won't. Every idol is an impostor. Jesus responds, "Those options are not true life." This is the first crucial moment—facing what the options really amount to and realizing "that's not really life." A deep, robust thirst – like we feel after a long, hot hike—can be quenched only by water. To be offered a hot fudge sundae wouldn't tempt us at all. And so we see the importance of entering into desire, of knowing full well what we're craving. (p. 172)

Will it work? Will that option really satisfy you . . . in the long run?

Of course not. I just end up stressed out, and I emerge hungrier than ever but less clear on what I want because I've been so distracted. It's actually phase one in a longer campaign to set me up for a deeper fall.

The second trial comes after we determine not to take matters into our own hands. By refusing to turn stones to bread, Jesus chooses to trust God. That is what we are saying when we refuse our options as well. Satan's reply is, "Oh, so you're going to trust your God. Fine. Prove he cares for you." He comes with an attack on God's heart toward us. This is almost inevitable for the thirsty soul. After we have chosen to remain in our thirst for a while, the doubts begin to creep in. *God, I know you love me. But I didn't expect I'd have to wait so long for what I desire.* We begin to wonder, *Do you care for me, God?* Satan jumps all over this, throwing fuel on the fire of our doubts. (p. 173)

What deep disappointment lingers in your life? What unmet desire, despite years of prayer? What have you been tempted to believe about God—and about yourself—because of that unmet desire?

Jesus' response is our only hope: "I don't need to prove that God cares for me. He cares for me *now*." There is no other place to stand . . . Jesus came to answer once and for all our question, "Do you care for me, God?" That is why the ground before the cross is the only place we can take a firm stand against the doubts that come in the journey of desire. We don't need for God to prove his love for us; he has, at the cross. (pp. 173–74)

Just try to hang on to this for the next ten days: "My heart matters to God." Hold it up, like a shield, against all other thoughts, doubts, feelings. "My heart matters to God." What do you begin to experience? (You'll need to let those days pass, of course, before you can answer this).

"You don't have to take the route of suffering," [Satan] says. "There are shortcuts. Just give your heart away." It all comes down to worship. What will we give our hearts away to, in return for the promise of life? May says this is "the ultimate invitation to idolatry." Jesus shuts Satan down: "There are no shortcuts, and my heart belongs to God alone."

Once we realize what a precious thing this is, the heart's desire, we must see that to guard it is worth our all. To neglect it is foolishness. To kill it is suicide. To allow it to wander aimlessly, to be trapped by the seductions of the evil one, is disaster. We must be *serious* about our happiness. (p. 174)

What is Satan trying to get you to do with your heart—kill it, or give it away? How will you respond to him?

TUNING THE INSTRUMENT

Holiness is not numbness; it is sensitivity. It is being *more* attuned to our desires, to what we were truly made for and therefore what we truly want. Our problem is that we've grown quite used to seeking life in all kinds of things other than God . . . [Gerald] May comments, "The more we become accustomed to seeking spiritual satisfaction through things other than God, the more abnormal and stressful it becomes to look for God directly." (pp. 175–76)

Do you find it hard to turn to God, to spend several hours with him, or a day, or even a weekend away, devoted to just being with God?

This is really helpful to remember. I often find it hard to turn to him, to just go be with him, break away from all that seems so important and spend an hour in silence and solitude. It's helpful to know it's OK, it's normal to feel like that, it takes time to make the switch. It allows me to be gentle with myself, while still insisting that I do turn to God and not just give up because it's hard.

Henri Nouwen once asked Mother Teresa for spiritual direction. Spend one hour each day in adoration of your Lord, she said, and never do anything you know is wrong. Follow this, and you'll be fine. Such simple, yet profound advice. Worship is the act of the abandoned heart adoring its God. It is the union that we crave. Few of us experience anything like this on a regular basis, let alone for an hour each day. But it is what we need. Desperately. Simply showing up on Sunday is not even close to worship. Neither does singing songs with religious content pass for worship. What counts is *the posture of the soul* involved, the open heart pouring forth its love toward God and communing with him. It is a question of desire.

Worship occurs when we say to God, from the bottom of our hearts, "You are the One whom I desire." (p. 177)

In your own words, what is worship—and what might look like the popular version, but is not worship at all?

Back in chapter eight we looked at how God gave us sex as the metaphor for true worship, for our union and communion with him. That metaphor will be helpful in seeing your way to a deeper intimacy with God. First, there is Courtship. Where do you find God? What has he used to woo your heart—has it been music? Beauty? Running in the early dawn? Sitting quietly by the window in the night? Lighting a fire in the fireplace and reading a good book? What has it been for you?

There you have it—go there, regularly, to be courted and to court God.

After a season of Courtship comes Vulnerability. We begin to share our true hearts with God; we open ourselves up to him and share from the depths of our truest self. What might help you do this? Would it be to journal? Shout? Cry? Bang on the steering wheel? Sing? Pray the psalms?

Do just that, and often.

After Vulnerability comes Communion—just being together, being one. It is the knowing and being known of lovers. Perhaps no words are necessary. Perhaps the words of God's other lovers will help you find a language of your own:

> There is nothing created that can fully satisfy my desires. Make me one with You in a sure bond of heavenly love, for You alone are sufficient to Your lover, and without You all things are vain and of no substance.

> Grant me, O most sweet and loving Jesus, to rest in thee above all creatures, above all health and beauty, above all glory and honor, above all power and dignity, above

all knowledge and subtlety, above all riches and arts, above all joy and gladness, above all fame and praise, above all sweetness and comfort, above all hope and promise, above all desert and desire . . .

Thou alone art most beautiful and loving, thou alone most noble and glorious above all things, in whom all good things together both perfectly are, and ever have been, and shall be. *(Thomas à Kempis)* (p. 178)

Close by writing out your prayer at this point in your journey.

LETTING GO

Grasp not at much for fear thou losest all.
—GEORGE HERBERT

For Jesus I have gladly suffered the loss of all things.
—THE APOSTLE PAUL

— Counsel for the Journey

This leg may be the most surprising . . . and the hardest. All along John and I have been encouraging you to uncover, discover, recover your heart's desire. We hope that has been going well for you.

Now in this section, you must wrestle with the idea of letting go, surrendering your desire to God. When I (Craig) think of "letting go," I focus on *what* it is I am letting go of. Is it an old refrigerator or my desire for a close friend's healing of a terminal disease? Letting go of an overused fridge is easy; letting go of a friend seems impossible. So to meaningfully speak of "letting go" is to enter the arena of strongly embraced possessions . . . those deeply rooted people and things that define life for us.

In order for your heart to live free, you must learn the spiritual grace of detachment—not abandoning your desire but surrendering your will. You are searching for the secret of hope—which Paul says involves groaning and waiting.

— Inspiration

John quoted David Wilcox's song "Slipping Through My Fist" in the corresponding chapter in the book, and if you haven't had a chance to listen to it, we think you'll find it haunting. It's on David's *Underneath* CD. Give it several hearings to really sink in, which won't be hard because it's such a beautiful song.

SETTING FORTH

I sat at the intersection staring dumbly at the barriers, the engine idling, cars piling up behind me. God began to speak to my sinking heart: *Your journey lies along another path. You've got to let all that go now.* I knew there was no arguing. I didn't even try to put up a fight. I've been known to plow through his barriers in the past, but not now. Remember checkmate? My grip has loosened in recent years, and I knew this was a call to loosen it even more . . .

One thing I have come to embrace is this: we have to let it go. (p. 180)

Were you surprised to find this idea of "letting go" in the journey of desire? What does it stir in you, on first pass?

To live in desire is to begin to taste joy indescribable, but much too brief. I (Craig) have had glimpses of life as it was meant to be, but they never last as long as I want. A couple of years ago I was overwhelmed with the beauty of a southern gentleman's "farm." I wrote the following in my journal: "Walking before sunrise, through forest, circling the pond with "Colt" the blue-heeler cattle dog, flushing out ducks from the water's edge. What is it about walking through the woods with a dog that's so enjoyable? The beauty of this farm is too much to take in . . . I know this is a once-in-a-lifetime experience, and I want to learn to enjoy it as such. When I see glory I want it to linger, linger in ways it won't (how long does a sunset last, a kiss, a child's smile, a victory . . . not long enough). Don't hold on tight, it won't last . . . let it slip through your fingers." Letting go is losing something and being surprised at what you gain.

The more comfortable we are with mystery in our journey, the more rest we will know along the way. (p. 180)

Are you comfortable with "mystery" being a part of life? Do you embrace life's mysteries or find yourself committed to eliminating them? Do you fight mystery or does it intrigue you or cause fear, frustration, anxiety?

Tracks of a Fellow Traveler

Visit a church on Sunday morning—almost any will do—and you will likely find a congregation comfortably relating to a deity who fits nicely within precise doctrinal positions, or who lends almighty support to social crusades, or who conforms to individual spiritual experiences. But you will not likely find much awe or sense of mystery. The only sweaty palms will be those of the preacher unsure whether the sermon will go over; the only shaking knees will be those of the soloist about to sing the offertory. (Donald W. McCullough, The Trivialization of God)

What mysteries compose your story?

It feels as though I could write out so much here . . . the mystery of my wife's love for me, the mystery of my heart wandering from God, lured away by distractions *and a tempter's wares . . . I always return, but why do I leave? God's grace and choice of me as his beloved are way beyond my ability to understand . . . a mystery.*

My father's death when I was an infant dramatically changed how my life would unfold (I've often thought of what might have been . . . and, of course, my picture is gloriously different from how it turned out).

The Christian path seems to involve so much more "groaning," aching, and battling than I, as a young Christian, ever envisioned as part of the journey . . . I wonder why God doesn't do things so very differently than he does (I continue to deepen my belief that he is good; I have no doubt that he is redemptive) . . . yet it seems he is often silent, distant, and it tragically appears the enemy is much more victorious than he ought to be . . . to me this is a mystery.

WILLING TO THIRST

There is a widespread belief in the church that to be a Christian somehow satisfies our every desire . . . What complete nonsense! Augustine emphasized, "The whole life of the good Christian is a holy longing. What you desire ardently, as yet you do not see." So, "let us long because we are to be filled . . . That is our life, to be exercised by longing." (p. 181)

What does living a whole life of longing elicit in you? Does that settle and resolve some of your expectations for life, or does it spin you into the "blues," into a cynicism or frustration of heart? To what degree have you, do you, expect your every desire to be satisfied?

I'd agree with Augustine—my whole life has been longing. For most of my life, and I still very much wrestle with this, I have lived in a small story, a story starring Me. The longings would be better described as demands, as expectations from life and those closest to me. All I've ever wanted is:

- A wife who makes me the center of the universe.

- Daughters who sit at my feet with deep-seated admiration, asking one question after the other of me about life, God, and how they might meet and marry a man like me (except that he is generously rich and willing to provide for his aging in-laws).

- An absence of earthquakes, crime, taxes, skin cancer, and all other life-threatening diseases.

- A place for everything and everything in its place.

- Two cars that run . . . one good suit, a great sound system, and a full head of hair.

- A circle of friends who intuitively know when to give me a call and when to give me a break; they know when to stop by and when to leave, encourage me when I need it, consider me their best friend but don't ask too much of me.

- A ministry in a church that, without drawing sinful attention to me, is on the cutting edge of a revival unknown since the book of Acts.

- A couple of weeks of vacation annually, two weeks on the Oregon coast, another in the mountains, several in Europe, Christmas in Seattle, Thanksgiving in New York, a few weekends in the desert and a week in a tropical paradise every other year.

JOURNEY OF DESIRE JOURNAL AND GUIDEBOOK

I'm joking—yet not fully. These are some of my desires (there are others, too, some deeper, truer, less tangled). It was only a few years ago that I began to understand there's another story, a story starring God . . . a larger story, much larger than my own. As that story captured me and as I find my place in it, I am both more desirous and more patient. I know that the next chapter holds more satisfaction for me than the present one.

Paul said he had "learned the secret of being content" (Phil. 4:12 NIV), and many Christians assume he no longer experienced the thirst of his soul. But earlier in the same epistle, the old saint said that he had *not* obtained his soul's desire, or "already been made perfect." Quite the contrary. He describes himself as pressing on, "straining toward what is ahead" (Phil. 3:12–14 NIV). These are not the words of a man who no longer experienced longing because he had arrived. They are the account of a man propelled on his life quest by his desire.

Contentment is not freedom *from* desire, but freedom *of* desire. Being content is not pretending that everything is the way you wish it would be; it is not acting as though you have no wishes. Rather, it is no longer being *ruled* by your desires. (pp. 181–82)

Does that change your idea of contentment? What did you think contentment was? And with this new view in mind, what would it look like for you to be content these days?

The fact is, at this point in our journey, we have only three options: (1) to be alive and thirsty, (2) to be dead, or (3) to be addicted. There are no other choices. (p. 182)

Given those three options: to be alive and thirsty, to be dead, or to be addicted, how would you describe yourself and how would those who know you well describe you? Why?

Most of the world lives in addiction; most of the church has chosen deadness. The Christian is called to the life of holy longing. But we don't like to stay there . . .

To live in thirst is to live with an ache. Every addiction comes from the attempt to get rid of the ache. How is it possible to satisfy an insatiable desire? Merely trying sets us on an unending chase that leads us farther and farther from home . . . You can be satisfied . . . you just can't be sated. (pp. 182, 183)

You can't get rid of the ache. What does that realization stir in you?

God grants us so much of our heart's desire as we delight in him: "You open your hand and satisfy the desires of every living thing" (Ps. 145:16 NIV). Not always, not on demand, but certainly more than we deserve. God delights to give good gifts to his beloved. But that old root would have us shift once more from giver to gift, and seek our rest through being full. This is the turn we must be vigilant to see, watching over our hearts with loving care. (p. 183)

What good gifts has God given you this past year?

WHAT HOPE FEELS LIKE

We know that the whole creation has been groaning as in the pains
of childbirth right up to the present time. Not only so, but we ourselves,
who have the firstfruits of the Spirit, groan inwardly as we wait eagerly
for our adoption as sons, the redemption of our bodies. For in this hope
we were saved. But hope that is seen is no hope at all. Who hopes for
what he already has? But if we hope for what we do not yet have, we wait
for it patiently. (Rom. 8:22–25 NIV)

Amazing. Paul is passing along to us the secret of the sojourning heart. We live in hope, and he says hoping is waiting. And groaning. (pp. 184–85)

Here is a simple question to ask yourself to see if you are a pilgrim or an arranger: What are you waiting for? Is there anything you ardently desire that you are doing nothing to secure?

WAITING

To wait is to learn the spiritual grace of *detachment*, the freedom of desire. Not the absence of desire, but desire at rest . . . The word *detachment* might evoke wrong impressions. This is not a cold and indifferent attitude; not at all. May writes, "An authentic spiritual understanding of detachment devalues neither desire nor the objects of desire." Instead, it "aims at correcting one's own anxious grasping in order to free oneself for committed relationship to God." (pp. 185, 186)

As Thomas à Kempis declared, "Wait a little while, O my soul, wait for the divine promise, and thou shalt have abundance of all good things in heaven." In this posture we discover that, indeed, we are expanded by longing. Something grows in us, a capacity if you will, for life and love and God. I think of Romans 8:24–25: "That is why waiting does not diminish us, any more than waiting diminishes a pregnant mother. We are enlarged in the waiting. We, of course, don't see what is enlarging us. But the longer we wait, the larger we become, and the more joyful our expectancy" (*The Message*). There is actually a sweet pain in longing if we will let it draw our hearts homeward. (pp. 186–87)

What do you have a hard time waiting for?

How has "waiting" enlarged you, or, how do you hope or suspect it will?

AND GROANING

When I turned away from those barriers to the Lamar Valley, I accepted that I could not recover what had been lost. Not yet. My journey now lies along another path. And so we retreated from the road over Dunraven Pass, left Yellowstone through the south gate, and descended down into the Tetons, staying there for several nights.

One morning I woke early and could not get back to sleep. My soul was agitated, restless. After what seemed like an hour of tossing and turning, I rose and slipped out of the cabin to take a walk. Waves of grief began to sweep over my soul. But it was not all about Brent or even primarily about him. His death was the lance that pierced the wound of all the ungrieved grief of my life. Sorrows from my marriage, from college days, from wounds I received as a child—all of them poured forth through this place of release. Why had I waited so many years to shed these tears? As I wept, I realized that Paul was absolutely right. How can we live without groaning? If we do not give our ache a voice, it doesn't go away. It becomes the undercurrent of our addictions. Pleasure becomes necessary in larger and larger doses, like morphine. (p. 187)

How comfortable are you with groaning? Does the faith community you belong to, those close to you, allow you to groan?

Are you uncomfortable with others groaning, grieving, coming to tears in your presence? How do you respond to another's groaning?

Are there any aches you haven't "given voice" to?

The paradox of grief is that it is healing; it somehow restores our souls, when all the while we thought it would leave us in despair. Control is the enemy; grief is our friend . . . When the ministry of the Messiah is described in Isaiah 61, comfort for those who mourn and healing for the brokenhearted are placed at the center of his mission. None of this makes sense until we admit our broken heartedness and give our sorrow a voice in mourning. Only then we will know his comfort. (p. 188)

> Those who sow in tears
> 　　will reap with songs of joy.
> He who goes out weeping,
> 　　carrying seed to sow,
> will return with songs of joy,
> 　　carrying sheaves with him. (Ps. 126:5–6 NIV)

How have you grieved over your losses in life? Did you grieve well—or did you minimize the pain and loss, deny it, or pretend to be unscathed by the pain?

Have you ever tasted the sweet comfort of the Messiah in your grief? Can you put some words to the strength, beauty, and hope of that comfort?

I believe we must add two spiritual disciplines to everyday life. The first is worship. We must adore God deliberately, regularly. The other is grief. We must allow a time for sorrow, to do our own personal sowing. I see no other way to care for our hearts.

Now making time to grieve might seem strange to you. "But I don't feel grief or sorrow at all." Just because we do not feel it doesn't mean it is not there. Our pleasant experience may be the result of the thousand distractions which fill our waking moments. Keirkegaard said that despair has become so rare not because the human race is doing suddenly better, but because we so effectively push it away. This is the "sickness unto death," to despair without ever despairing, to mourn without ever mourning. (pp. 189–90)

Do you understand why John recommended these two "spiritual disciplines" for your life?

Can you see yourself adding these two disciplines to your life? How?

I've found, therefore, that quite often grief has to sneak up on us, surprise us during our day. It may come through a song you hear or a movie you see. It may come as you choose to allow your soul twenty minutes of quiet during your lunch hour. Sometimes a small disappointment can be the door into a room of grief you never knew was there. However unexpectedly grief shows up, let us accept it as a welcome visitor. (p. 190)

How has grief "snuck up" on you lately? Has anything nearly brought you to tears . . . and did you welcome them?

I'd counseled people about the vital need to grieve, yet I had never personally grieved the enormous loss of my father. Once I began, thirty-five years of anger, hurt, and shame poured out of me. The immediate feeling was an experience of dissonance because though he was killed thirty-five years ago, it felt as if it was only a moment ago. It was as though someone had just informed me that my father has just been killed. From that point on, and still, movies (Frequency, Legends of the Fall, the opening of Born on the Fourth of July, Pearl Harbor, Glory, etc.) uncork me; Hallmark card commercials, sweeping dramatic sound tracks, and military cemeteries stir the loss and my comfort. It can strike at any time . . . I cannot live without grieving, without being comforted as only Christ can.

LET BEAUTY HAVE ITS SAY

What can I possibly say to her? How can I begin to restore hope to her life? This is what was going through my mind as I listened to Kathleen. It was partly about being raped, and partly about the tensions in her marriage remaining years after, that she had come to see me. I wondered, *What can I offer this woman? What can I say to one who has known such terrible evil?* We sat in my office on a cold winter afternoon; outside all was gray. Perhaps that's the reason I first noticed the little flowers embroidered on the collar of her denim shirt. As she told me her tragic story, my eye kept coming back to those graceful little bouquets. Maybe I was surprised by them, but somehow I felt they were the clue to her restoration. Kathleen finished her story, and we sat in silence. After a few moments, I couldn't help mentioning the flowers. "Oh," she said. "Ever since the rape, beauty has meant the world to me. No one seemed to understand why. Sometimes I would spend hours just gazing at my garden and the woods behind my house. Only beauty helps." (pp. 190–91)

Can you recall times in your journey when beauty meant the world to you?

I understand completely. As the shock of Brent's death began to wear off, the searing pain of intense grief took its place. It was too difficult to read my Bible. Conversation required more than I was able to give. Frankly, I didn't want to talk to anyone, not even God. The only thing that helped was my wife's flower garden. The solace I found there was like nothing else on earth. I wrote in my journal, *Sitting outside this evening, the Shasta daisies swaying in the gentle breeze on their long stems, the aspens shimmering without light, the full moon rising over the pine crested bluff . . . only beauty speaks what I need to hear. Only beauty helps.*

Simone Weil was absolutely right—beauty and affliction are the only two things that can pierce our hearts. Because this is so true, we must have a measure of beauty in our lives proportionate to our affliction. No, more. Much more. Is this not God's prescription for us? Just take a look around. The sights and sounds, the aromas and sensations—the world is overflowing with beauty. God seems to be rather enamored with it. Gloriously wasteful. Apparently, he feels that there ought to be plenty of it in our lives. (p. 191)

How, or where, can you take in beauty this week? Where in your daily living can you go to find beauty?

"We have had a couple of inspiring sunsets this week." A dear friend sent this in an E-mail. "It was as if the seams of our atmosphere split for a bit of heaven to plunge into the sea. I stood and applauded . . . simultaneously I wanted to kneel and weep." Yes—that's it. All I want to do is validate those irreplaceable moments, lift any obstacle you may have to filling your life with greater and greater amounts of beauty.

We need not fear indulging here. The experience of beauty is unique to all the other pleasures in this: there is no possessive quality to it. Just because you love the landscape doesn't mean you have to acquire the real estate. Simply to behold the flower is enough; there is nothing in me that wants to consume it. Beauty is the closest thing we have to fullness without possessing on this side of eternity. It heralds the Great Restoration. Perhaps that is why it is so healing—beauty is pure gift. It helps us in our letting go. (p. 192)

How can you begin to fill your life with more beauty? Is it more music, art, nature—what?

SURRENDER

Tracks of a Fellow Traveler

God comes and offers to work this absolute surrender in you. All these searchings and hungering and longings that are in your heart, I tell you they are the drawings of the divine magnet, Christ Jesus. He lived a life of absolute surrender, He has possession of you; He is living in your heart by His Holy Spirit. You have hindered and hindered Him terribly, but He desires to help you to get hold of Him entirely. And He comes and draws you now by His message and words. Will you not come and trust God to work in you that absolute surrender to Himself? Yes, blessed be God, He can do it, and He will do it. (Andrew Murray, Absolute Surrender)

The time has come for us to quit playing chess with God over our lives. We cannot win, but we can delay the victory, dragging on the pain of grasping and the poison of possessing. You see, there are two kinds of losses in life. The first is shared by all mankind—the losses that come to us. Call them what you will—accidents, fate, acts of God. The point is that we have no control over them. We do not determine when, where, what, or even how. There is no predicting these losses; they happen *to* us. We only choose how we respond. (pp. 192–93)

What would you count as "losses that came to you" in your life? How did you respond?

The second kind of loss is known only to the pilgrim. They are losses that we *choose*. A chosen loss is different from repentance, when we give up something that was never ours to have. With a chosen loss, we place on the altar something very dear to us, something innocent, whose only danger is in its goodness, that we might come to love it too much. It is the act of *consecration*, where little by little or all at once, we give over our lives to the only One who can truly keep them.

Spiritual surrender is not resignation. It is not choosing to care no longer. Nor is it Eastern mysticism, an attempt to get beyond the suffering of this life by going completely numb. As my dear friend Jan describes, "It is surrender *with* desire, or *in* desire." Desire is still present, felt, welcomed even. But the will to secure is made subject to the divine will in an act of abandoned trust. (p. 193)

Looking back, what would you record as a "chosen loss"?

And what might you need to choose to give up in this next season of your journey? Where in your life are you being called to live with a desire you cannot—or should not—arrange for?

Christ is weeping freely; his prayers are marked by loud cries and tears. He makes it very, very clear what he desires. Not once, but three times he begs his Father to remove this awful cup from him: "Yet not my will, but thine be done." He surrenders with desire, in desire. Making himself poor, he opens up to us the treasures of heaven. Buddha abandons his desire; Christ surrenders his will. It is no small difference.

True surrender is not an easy out, calling it quits early in the game. This kind of surrender comes only *after* the night of wrestling. It comes only after we open our hearts to care deeply. Then we choose to surrender, or give over, our deepest desires to God. And with them we give over our hearts, our deepest selves. The freedom and beauty and rest that follow are among the greatest of all surprises . . .

I tasted this wonderful freedom a few months ago, canoeing on a high mountain lake. My boys had already gone in for the day, and so I was alone in the canoe, paddling across this beautiful lake at dusk. That's when the trout began to rise. The surface of the water was serene in the little cove I had found, and the dimples made by feeding rainbows were too numerous to count. It is the moment fly fishermen dream about. I set down the paddle and picked up my rod to begin casting. As the line unfurled, my fly alighted gently on the water in the middle of a dozen rise-rings. First one, then two trout took my offering. I knew that if the fish continued to rise, I would have my fill before it became too dark to fish anymore. But then, a gentle breeze began to blow down the valley. It was cool and fragrant and refreshing, and though it was soft, I noticed it was strong enough to carry my canoe along. A tremor of anxiety passed through me, for I knew I could not fish and paddle at the same time. To stay in this little cove, among the rising trout, I would have to put down the rod and pick up the paddle.

I smiled and set down the rod. But I didn't take up the paddle. I let my hands rest along the gunwales and let the gentle breeze take me away, out across the surface of the lake. And as I drifted, I drank in the beauty of the mountain peaks around me, and the golden quality of the fading light, and the joy of the freedom of my desire. A little voice reminded me that fish were rising back in the cove.

> But I was wondering where the wind was trying to take me
> overnight, if I never did resist, and
> what strange breezes make a sailor want to
> let it come to this,
> with lines untied, slipping through my fist.
> (pp. 194–95)

If you were to let go, where might God take you? Are you willing to go?

Write out the prayer of your heart in response to this chapter.

KEEPING HEART—TO THE END

Remember thee!
Yea, from the table of my memory
I'll wipe away all trivial fond records . . .
And thy commandment all alone shall live
Within the book and volume of my brain
Unmix'd with baser matter.
—HAMLET

Sometimes I wake, and, lo, I have forgot.
—GEORGE MACDONALD

But every now and anon a trumpet sounds from the hid
battlements of eternity.
—FRANCIS THOMPSON

— Counsel for the Journey

Well, dear pilgrim, our journey together is nearly at an end. In this last leg
that I (John) will provide some guidance for, I want you to consider carefully
how you will not lose heart. What will you cling to? What "Rule" will you
adopt for your life? What treasures must you hide away? And most important,
can you see where the adventure is leading you next . . . and will you follow?

This is preparation for the journey ahead.

— Inspiration

The dilemma of desire, the fear that comes with this last chapter, and the
freedom of finally following what is written on your heart by God are all
contained in a Bebo Norman song called "Tip of My Heart," from the *Big Blue*

Sky CD. We think you'll love it. (I quote a few lines at the close of this chapter.)

And, now that you've come this far, we can recommend the film *Chocolat*. It's a powerful picture of the suffocating nature of religion as duty, and the redemptive power of recovered desire. If only the heroine were depicted as a messenger of true Christianity; apart from that, it's a parable of this book in many ways.

We haven't heard from the sea lion lately. Do you miss him? What do you suppose he's up to? Try your hand at writing a passage about him now—perhaps as a parable of your own life and journey at this point.

OUR WORST ENEMY

Forgetting is no small problem. Of all the enemies our hearts must face, this may be the worst because it is so insidious. Forgetfulness does not come against us like an enemy in full battle formation, banners waving. Nor does it come temptingly, seductively, the lady in red. It works slowly, commonly, unnoticed. My wife had a beautiful climbing rose vine that began to fill an arbor in her garden. We enjoyed the red blossoms it produced every summer. But last year, something happened. The vine suddenly turned brown, dropped its flowers, and died within the course of a week. After all that loving care we couldn't figure out what went wrong. A call to the nursery revealed that a worm had gotten into the stalk of the vine and eaten away at the life from the inside. Such is the work of forgetfulness. It cuts us off from our Life so slowly, we barely notice, until one day the blooms of our faith are suddenly gone. (p. 200)

Would you have thought that forgetfulness was that big an issue—let alone your worst enemy?

The first time I read [the story about the people of Macando] I simply laughed. But it haunted me, and on a second reading I began to realize that it's my story too. I said to myself, *It's not a bad plan. Right above my bed I think I shall hang a sign that says,* GOD EXISTS. You see, I wake most mornings an unbeliever. It seems that during the night, I slip into forgetfulness, and by the time the new day comes, I am lost. The deep and precious truths that God has brought to me over the years and even just yesterday seem a thousand miles away. It doesn't happen every morning, but enough to make it an ongoing reality. And I know I am not alone in this. (p. 199)

Can you relate? Do you wake each morning with a rich and full memory of all God has done and spoken in the past? Or are you like Chuck Colson, who once said that he's an atheist until he has a cup of coffee?

If you don't think forgetting is a deep problem, then do this: write down here the many answers to prayer that God has given you in just the past year.

Better still, read through an old journal of yours. Rediscover a time in your life when God really showed up, came through, or spoke to you in a meaningful way. (This exercise will do wonders for your faith.) What is it like to *remember* that?

BE FOREWARNED

We're certainly warned about forgetfulness in Scripture, both in word and by example. In the Old Testament, the pattern is so predictable, we come to expect it. God delivers his people from the cruel whips of Egypt by a stunning display of his power and his care—the plagues, the Passover, the Red Sea. The Israelites celebrate with singing and dancing. Three days later, they are complaining about the water supply. God provides sweet water from the bitter desert springs of Marah. They complain about the food. God drops breakfast out of the sky, every morning. Then it's the water again. God provides it from a rock. Enemies attack; God delivers. On and on it goes, for forty years. As they stand on the brink of the promised land, God issues a final warning: "Only be careful, and watch yourselves closely so that you do not forget the things your eyes have seen or *let them slip from your heart* as long as you live" (Deut. 4:9 NIV, emphasis added).

They do, of course, let it slip from their hearts. All of it. This becomes the pattern for the entire history of Israel. God shows up; he does amazing things; the people rejoice. Then they forget and go whoring after other gods. They fall under calamity and cry out for deliverance. God shows up; he does amazing things; the people rejoice—you get the picture. Round and round and round we go; where she stops, nobody knows. And like the people of Macondo, their story is our story. (pp. 200–201)

What have been the cycles of your walk with God over the past six months? Has it been steady, even, ever upward? Or do you fall back into old, abiding places? What are they? Describe the cycle.

WHAT WILL WE CLING TO?

Life is a journey of the heart that requires the mind—not the other way around. The church sometimes gets this backward and makes knowing the right things the center of life. It's not; the heart is the center of life. Desire is always where the action is. However, staying alive to our desire is not enough; we know that only too well. We must bring the *truth* into our hearts to guard and to guide our desire; this is the other half of our mission. (p. 202)

Put the journal down and say this to yourself, slowly, five times: "Life is a journey of the heart that requires the mind." What arises in your soul?

With a recovery of heart and soul taking place in many quarters, my fear now is that we will abandon the pursuit of truth and try to base our journey on our feelings and intuition. "Follow your heart" is becoming a popular message in our culture. Or as Sting sings, "Trust your soul." It will not work. Our spiritual fathers and mothers knew this only too well. In *The Imitation of Christ*, à Kempis warned, "Our own opinion and our own sense do often deceive us, and they discern but little." We must cling to the truth for dear life. (p. 202)

What truths have you been clinging to for dear life? And if the question embarrasses you, if you don't cling to certain truths really that much in your day-to-day life, what does that say about how you are caring for your heart?

That my heart is good—this is the truth I(John) have really been trying to hang with. I have a new heart. My heart is "circumcised to God" (Rom. 2:29). Yesterday felt like a breakthrough, like it was finally sinking in. There was a new joyfulness about me and a freedom to speak into the lives of others. Then last night it was brutal battle. Man, it's hard to cling.

Now, not all truths help us descend with the mind into the heart. There is a way of talking about the truth that can actually deaden our hearts . . .

What is the truth of a kiss? Technically, in a modernistic sense, it is two sets of mandibles pressing together for a certain duration of time. Those of you who have experienced the wonders of a kiss will know that while true, this description is so untrue. It takes away everything beautiful and mysterious and passionate and intimate and leaves you with an icy cold fact. Those who know kissing feel robbed; those who don't are apt to say, "If that's what kissing is all about, I think I'd rather not."

We've done the same thing to theology. We have dissected God, and man, and the gospel, and we have thousands, if not millions, of facts—all of it quite dead. It's not that these insights aren't true; it's that they no longer speak . . . We must return to the Scriptures for the story that it is and stop approaching it as if it is an encyclopedia, looking for "tips and techniques." (pp. 203–4)

What is your approach to the Bible? Does it read like one of your favorite movies—an epic like *Braveheart* or *Titanic*—or does it feel like the yellow pages?

And how do the Christians in your church approach the Bible? Do they bring away tips and techniques, duty and information? Or do they find themselves swept up in a Great Drama, "a desperate quest through dangerous country to a destination that is, beyond all our wildest hopes, indescribably good"?

Reminders of the story are everywhere—in films and novels, in children's fairy tales, in the natural world around us, and in the stories of our own lives. In fact, every story or movie or song or poem that has ever stirred your soul is telling you something you need to know about the Sacred Romance. Even nature is crying out to us of God's great heart and the drama that is unfolding. Sunrise and sunset tell the tale every day, remembering Eden's glory, prophesying Eden's return. These are the trumpet calls from the "hid battlements of eternity." We must capture them like precious treasures and hold them close to our hearts. (p. 204)

This will change your life. Has it occurred to you that every movie you love and every song that stirs your heart is telling you about God and the gospel?

Make a list of your favorite stories right now—films, novels, fairy tales. Next to them, write down *why* you love them.

Now—can you see the themes of the gospel in those stories? Is it a great battle to be fought? Is it a story of undying love? Ask God to reveal to your heart what he has been speaking to you through those very stories.

Let me give you two examples. First is the film The Matrix. It depicts an entire world held captive to evil—and they don't even know it. Most people assume that the physical world they see is all there is. But that is not all there is. A fierce battle rages for their freedom, and the forces of good are small and brave and spend their lives trying to set the captives free. Finally, the hero, Neo ("the chosen one"), must die in the Matrix to break its power. The whole film is based on the *gospel, and a far more powerful and realistic look at the Christian life and mission than you'll encounter most Sunday mornings. The second example is from the film Gladiator, also based on the gospel. "A general becomes a slave, a slave becomes a gladiator, a gladiator defies an empire." Isn't Jesus, the Lord of Hosts, the general of angel armies? But when he came to earth he came as a slave, a bondservant. Yet he did not come to bring peace, but a sword, right? And he defies an empire, he pulls down the kingdom of darkness. I love that movie.*

How to Cling

We must be more intentional about holding on to the truth. (p. 205)

Do you have a plan? What will you *do* to cling to the truth?

Now, I'm not suggesting that we all adopt the Rule of Benedict. But think about this: these men left the distractions of the world to focus entirely on God. They lived in an environment *designed* to keep them standing before God, and what did they discover? They needed reminders every hour of the day and night! Do we, who live in the hostile chaos of the world, think we can do with an occasional visit? "Hey, Lord. I know it's been a while, but . . . um . . . thanks for being here and please help me get through this day." We are kidding ourselves if we think we can keep heart without a constant turning to the truth. (p. 206)

Do you have a rule of spiritual discipline to your life? Is there any "method to your madness," or do you sort of drop in for an occasional visit? Describe the spiritual disciplines of your past week.

Is your method working? Is your heart alive and free? Is your communion with God deepening?

So let me suggest a bit of monastic wisdom for contemporary pilgrims. First, you must reduce the constant noise of your life. Turn off the television; it is an enemy of your heart. Having one is like inviting *Vanity Fair* to set up shop in your home. The whole operation runs on mimetic passion, a continual assault on your desire. Even the news is a problem because of its artificial importance. Have you noticed? Every night there's such urgency to the stories; that's what they have to do to sell the news. But if everything is urgent, then nothing is. I believe Thoreau said, "Don't read the *Times*; read the eternities." Given the pace of our lives, I doubt we have room for both. Simply unplug from all the clamor, and make room for eternity in your life. In *The Wisdom of the Desert*, Thomas Merton reminds us of the early Christians who fled to the deserts south of Palestine in order to draw near to God. They saw society "as a shipwreck from which every single man had to swim for his life." They believed that to "let oneself drift along, passively accepting the tenets and values of what they knew as society, was purely and simply a disaster." (pp. 206–7)

How can you reduce the noise of your life? Can you unplug the television? Turn off the radio in your car? What is your plan for getting some silence and solitude into your life?

TREASURES FOR OUR HEARTS

After the shepherds learn about the birth of Christ from the angels, they seek and find the Babe, lying in a manger. The whole village is astounded by their report, but Mary, we are told, "treasured up all these things and pondered them in her heart" (Luke 2:19 NIV). Later, when the boy Jesus is found in the temple holding forth with the religious leaders, we are told again that everyone is quite amazed. "But his mother treasured all these things in her heart" (Luke 2:51 NIV). It is more than a touching story of a mother's love; Mary is going to need those treasures when the tide turns against her son. At her darkest hour, when a sword pierces her soul, she does not lose heart. I believe this is why.

So, if you do not have a way of seizing what God is speaking to you, begin journaling. Each year I take up a new journal in which to capture my heart's journey. *Journals* chronicle *journeys*; this is far different from simply recording the day's events in a diary, or worse still, the weekly goal sheets of the popular schedulers. A journal is about the interior life. (p. 207)

Do you journal regularly? If not, will you begin? Go to a bookstore and find a blank journal that expresses your taste and style. Then set aside several times a week to begin putting down your thoughts, writing out your prayers, capturing the things God is showing you.

If you do journal regularly, how can you enrich the experience? Do you revisit old journals, review what's happened, pick up themes and lessons learned? Another way might be to add photos, pictures from magazines, poems, quotes to your own journaling. Make it a treasury.

Tracks of a Fellow Traveler

But experience, no matter how accurately [expressed], can never furnish its own interpretation . . . Only when our experiences are situated within their larger theological context can we begin to grasp their spiritual import and ultimate meaning. (Julia Gatta)

At the back [of my journal] there is a section I have entitled "This New Day." There I am writing the central truths I must return to each morning (at least) to guide my desire home. My journal will be filled with all the twists and turns a year can bring, but here is the place I can go for the *interpretation* of the events and emotions and experiences. Like the Benedictines, we must keep before us the deepest truths— morning, noon, and night. (p. 207)

What are you using to *interpret* the events of your life, the unfolding drama? Can you make time to do it several times a week? It is vital that it not be rushed. The setting is important as well—it must quiet and focus your heart, not provide more distraction. Where will you go, when will you go, and what will you do?

GOD IS SPEAKING

As my friend Craig and I sat in the warm sun, eating lunch beside Four Mile Canyon, he picked up Pascal and read these words out loud: "It is awful to feel that everything we possess is hastening away, and to persist in our attachment, without being anxious, to examine if there is no object attainable that will be permanent." It was Thursday afternoon; that evening, our men's retreat was to begin. We had come up early to fish and to scout the area we would use for our rock-climbing sessions. Brent and the other guys would meet us later at the ranch.

The canyon is a beautiful place, with a lovely creek meandering through a meadow, framed on both sides by the high rock walls. It seemed strange to be talking about life slipping away when so much promise was in the air. A wonderful weekend lay ahead with some great men, doing the things I love best. I did not know why Craig had opened the *Pensées*, nor did I know the real story that was about to unfold. I would later realize that these were prophetic words, spoken to us by God at the opening of a very different scene.

God is speaking to us more often than we imagine. These are the treasures we must hide in our own hearts—sew them into our jackets if need be—for the dark hours that may come. (pp. 207–8)

God is speaking to us more often than we imagine. Oh, what a difference it would make if we could only see this more clearly. Think back over the past month or so. What events, conversations, movies, music, Scriptures have stirred you, troubled you, or in some way seemed to be laden with meaning (even if you don't know what the meaning is)? Write them down here. Then ask God to reveal to you what he is saying through those things. A prayer like this might help:

> *Oh Holy Spirit, you have come to lead me into all truth, to reveal to me the things of God (John 16:12–15). You reveal deep and hidden things; you know what lies in darkness, and light dwells with you (Dan. 2:22). Awaken me morning by morning, awaken my ear like one being taught (Isa. 50:4). Reveal to me what you are speaking through these events in my life. Enable me to hear and understand your voice more clearly. I ask in Jesus' name.*

And when he reveals that, write it down.

The story continues. This simple statement reminds me that life is unfolding, that we are headed somewhere, that the story is moving toward its happy ending. "What's past is prologue," as Shakespeare said. No event is the final word. Several weeks after Brent died, as I was walking from my car to my office, I said to myself, *The story has taken a tragic turn.* Somehow it mattered immensely to say it this way because it reminded me of all the tragic stories I have known and how they made me feel, how the heroes of those stories faced their tragedies, and so it gave weight to what I was living through. But it also kept me from despair because I found the moment in its context, not a random event but as Brent would often say, "A love affair in the midst of a life-and-death struggle." I was able to allow my heart to know it is not the end—the story continues. Dan Allender notes, "Faith increases to the degree we are aware of, caught up in, enthralled by, and participating in His and our story." (pp. 208–9)

Every moment in our lives is like a scene from a movie—every life, for that matter, is like a chapter from a novel. It makes no sense without the rest of the story! Do you see your life as part of a Great Story, a Sacred Romance, a love affair set in the midst of a life-and-death struggle?

If not, it may help you to read *The Sacred Romance* by Brent Curtis and John Eldredge, or perhaps *Telling the Truth: The Gospel as Tragedy, Comedy, and Fairy Tale* by Frederick Buechner, or *Orthodoxy* by G. K. Chesterton.

> *It can't be done.* By this I remember that I can't arrange for the life I prize. I am not fully healed yet of my addictions and my tendency—which seems so second nature—to arrange for my own little Eden now. To say again and again, "It can't be done," does not discourage me; quite the contrary, it frees my heart from the grasping and plotting and fretting over my life, which always accompany arranging. It reminds me to let it go. It breaks the power of the spell the evil one is trying to weave around us. (p. 209)

What are the issues in your life that you are still trying to control? Where is it you are still trying to arrange for your little Eden here? What is it you are most deeply having a hard time trusting God over?

Now you know where God will be working with you, in you, to set your heart more truly free.

> *It is coming.* Oh, how I forget this most of all. How easy it is to slip back into thinking that it's now or never; that if it's not here, it's not at all. The life I prize is coming. The very thing that I am aching for now, missing now, seeking now in other things is exactly what's coming to me. This is how I interpret the promises that seem to be coming through the good and beautiful gifts we have now. As you raise your glass of wine, toast to the banquet to come; as you see anything beautiful you'd like to have . . . say to yourself, *In a little while it shall be mine forever;* as you make love, remember

it is rehearsal for the Grand Affair. That way your heart will not be trapped there. I recall the end of MacDonald's novel *Phantastes*: "A great good is coming—is coming—is coming to thee." (p. 209)

Are you living with a deeper awareness that the life you were made for, the secret of your heart, really and truly *is* coming? What are the remaining doubts? And what stirs your hope that it is true?

The doubts are what we bring to God in prayer, so that he may speak to them. The reminders that stir hope are the things you should paste in your journal, watch again, or revisit.

> *Battle and journey.* We are at war, and the bloody battle is over our hearts. I am astounded how few Christians see this, how little they protect their hearts. We act as though we live in a sleepy little town during peacetime. We don't. We live in the spiritual equivalent of Bosnia or Beirut. Act like it. Watch over your heart. Don't let just anything in; don't let it go just anywhere. *What's this going to do to my heart?* is a question that I ask in every situation. (p. 210)

What are the latest assaults on your heart? Are you aware of them? How will you live as if you are at war? What will you do to protect your heart?

And thinking of journey reminds me to stop trying to set up camp and call it home. It allows me to see life as process, with completion somewhere down the road. Thus I am freed from feeling like a failure when things are not finished, and hopeful that they will be as my journey comes to its end. I want adventure, and this reminds me I am living in it. Life is not a problem to be solved; it is an adventure to be lived. (p. 210)

Life is now an adventure, and one of the greatest adventures before you is to follow your heart's desire. What risks do you need to take? What desires need to be pursued? After all the work you've done here, what needs to change about your life?

Is there a closing prayer you'd like to write out here?

Tracks of a Fellow Traveler

So I'm gonna live, I'm gonna love
I'm not afraid because your grace will always be enough
I'm gonna laugh, I'm gonna be set free
And let You hold all that my soul has deep inside of me
You have shown me where to start
It's on the tip of my heart.

(Bebo Norman, "Tip of My Heart" from the record Big Blue Sky by Watershed Records, an imprint
of Essential Records, distributed by Provident Music Distribution. Copyright © 2001 New Spring
Publishing, Inc./AppStreet Publishing, Inc./ASCAP. All rights administered by Brentwood-Benson Music
Publishing, Inc. All rights reserved.)

ABOUT THE AUTHOR

John Eldredge is an author, counselor, and lecturer. For twelve years he was a writer and speaker for Focus on the Family, most recently serving on the faculty of the Focus on the Family Institute. Now John is director of Ransomed Heart™ Ministries, a teaching, counseling, and discipling fellowship devoted to helping people recover and live from their deep hearts. John lives in Colorado Springs with his wife, Stasi, and their three sons. He loves living in Colorado so he can pursue his other passions, including fly-fishing, mountain climbing, and exploring the waters of the West in his canoe.

To learn more about John's seminars, audiotapes, and other resources for the heart, visit his Web site, www.RansomedHeart.com, or write to:

Ransomed Heart™
P.O. Box 51065
Colorado Springs, CO 80949-1065

OTHER BOOKS FROM JOHN ELDREDGE

THE SACRED ROMANCE:
Drawing Closer to the Heart of God
With Brent Curtis

This life-changing book has guided hundreds of thousands of readers from a busyness-based religion to a deeply felt relationship with the God who woos you. As you draw closer to Him, you must choose to let go of other "less-wild lovers," such as perfectionistic drivenness and self-indulgence, and embark on your own journey to recover the lost life of your heart and with it the intimacy, beauty, and adventure of life with God.

Trade Paper Edition—ISBN 0-7852-7342-5
Special Collector's Edition (Hardcover)—ISBN 0-7852-6723-9
Abridged Audio—ISBN 0-7852-6786-7

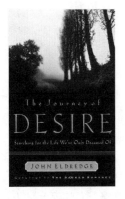

THE JOURNEY OF DESIRE:
Searching for the Life We've Only Dreamed Of

Author Dan Allender calls *The Journey of Desire* "a profound and winsome call to walk into the heart of God." This life-changing book picks up where *The Sacred Romance* leaves off and continues the journey. In it, John Eldredge invites you to abandon resignation, to rediscover your God-given desires, and to search again for the life you once dreamed of.

Hardcover Edition—ISBN 0-7852-6882-0
Trade Paper Edition—ISBN 0-7852-6716-6

THE SACRED ROMANCE WORKBOOK AND JOURNAL:
Your Personal Guide to Drawing Closer to the Heart of God

The Sacred Romance Workbook and Journal is a guided journey of the heart featuring exercises, journaling, and the arts to usher you into an *experience*—the recovery of your heart and the discovery of your life as part of God's great romance.

ISBN 0-7852-6846-4

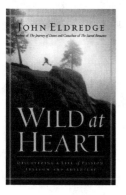

WILD AT HEART:
Discovering the Secret of a Man's Soul

Every man was once a boy. And every little boy has dreams, big dreams. But what happens to those dreams when they grow up? Walk into most churches and have a look around. You'll find that most Christian men are . . . bored. In *Wild at Heart*, John Eldredge invites men to recover their masculine heart, defined in the image of a passionate God. And he invites women to discover the secret of a man's soul and to delight in the strength and wildness men were created to offer.

ISBN 0-7852-6883-9

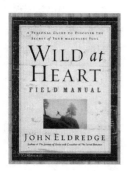

WILD AT HEART FIELD MANUAL:
A Personal Guide to Discover the Secret of Your Masculine Soul

Abandoning the format of workbooks-as-you-know-them, the *Wild at Heart Field Manual* will take you on a journey through which John Eldredge gives you permission to be what God designed you to be—dangerous, passionate, alive, and free. Filled with questions, exercises, personal stories from readers, wide-open writing spaces to record your "field notes," this book will lead you on a journey to discover the masculine heart that God gave you.

ISBN 0-7852-6574-0

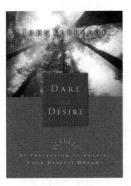

DARE TO DESIRE:
An Invitation to Fulfill Your Deepest Dreams

Dare to Desire is the perfect book if you are ready to move beyond the daily grind to a life overflowing with adventure, beauty, and a God who loves you more passionately than you dared imagine. With brand-new content as well as concepts from *The Sacred Romance, The Journey of Desire,* and *Wild at Heart,* John Eldredge takes you on a majestic journey through the uncharted waters of the human heart.

Printed Hardcover Gift Book

With Beautiful, Full-Color Design

from J. Countryman, a division of Thomas Nelson, Inc.

ISBN 0-8499-9591-4